"Tora, tora, tora!" – never in history has the outbreak of war so shattered the world as when Japan attacked Pearl Harbour on 8th December, 1941. Within minutes, America had suffered her worst military defeat. Her proud Pacific fleet had been smashed and sunk; Japan's might seemed to overshadow the whole Far East.

This book re-enacts the events that led up to this fateful December morning, and describes the air attack and its immediate aftermath. Key documents and eyewitness accounts are used to underline the tragedy, and the reasons for Japan's success. They also place the Pearl Harbour attack in the wider context of Japanese aims and military moves in the Far East.

Roger Parkinson has chosen a fascinating selection of sources from America, Britain and Japan. National policies and actions are juxtaposed to show the false hopes and eleventh-hour attempts of Washington and London to fight off war. The author includes the official American Hearings on Pearl Harbour, the incredible and frightening minutes of Tokyo's Liaison Conferences, and minutes of Churchill's War Cabinet. The latter have only recently been released from security classification, and some of the extracts used are now published for the first time.

In addition to the gripping exchanges of the diplomats, the author gives the military background; the training, planning and execution of the attack on Pearl Harbour.

Frontispiece The U.S. Navy destroyers *Downes* and *Cassin* lie devastated after the Japanese bombing of Pearl Harbour

Attack on Pearl Harbour

Roger Parkinson

"Tora, tora, tora!" – *"Tiger, tiger, tiger!"* – The victory signal of the Japanese pilots at Pearl Harbour, 8th December, 1941.

In this series
ATTACK ON PEARL HARBOUR   *R. Parkinson*
BATTLE OF THE SOMME   *C. Martin*
BATTLE OF THE SPANISH ARMADA   *Roger Hart*
THE BLACK DEATH AND PEASANT'S REVOLT   *Leonard Cowie*
THE BRITISH RAJ   *Denis Judd*
GLADSTONE AND DISRAELI   *Patrick Rooke*
THE GREAT DEPRESSION   *Marion Yass*
GUNPOWDER, TREASON AND PLOT   *Lewis Winstock*
HIROSHIMA   *Marion Yass*
THE HOME FRONT   *Marion Yass*
ITALY UNDER MUSSOLINI   *Christopher Leeds*
MEDIEVAL PILGRIMS   *Alan Kendall*
ORIGINS OF WORLD WAR ONE   *R. Parkinson*
ORIGINS OF WORLD WAR TWO   *R. Parkinson*
PLAGUE AND FIRE   *Leonard Cowie*
THE REFORMATION OF THE SIXTEENTH CENTURY   *Leonard Cowie*
RUSSIA UNDER STALIN   *Michael Gibson*
THE THIRD REICH   *Michael Berwick*
THE VIKINGS   *Michael Gibson*
WITCHCRAFT   *Roger Hart*

Cover: A painting by Norman Wilkinson showing the aftermath of the Japanese attack on Pearl Harbour.
Frontispiece: The U.S. Navy destroyers *Downes* and *Cassin* lie devastated after the Japanese bombing of Pearl Harbour.

First published in 1973 by
Wayland (Publishers) Ltd
61 Western Road, Hove
East Sussex BN3 1JD

© Copyright 1973 Wayland (Publishers) Ltd

Second impression 1988

ISBN 1 85210 593 3

Printed and bound at
The Bath Press, Avon, England

Contents

The Illustrations

1 Tiger! Tiger!

AT 7 A.M. a shrill voice interrupted the scheduled Japanese radio broadcast. The people of Tokyo listened with astonishment. "At midnight today, the 8th December, our Army and Navy have opened hostilities with American and British forces." A statement by the Emperor Hirohito himself would be made later in the morning, proclaiming a war which would light the whole of the Far East in a blaze of barbaric cruelty, horror and fearful land, sea and air combat.

The shock of war

Japan had made her desperate bid for military glory and world conquest. And already, on this crisp December day in 1941, her green-clad troops were pushing and hacking their way through the jungles of British Malaya. Singapore had been bombed. Japanese aircraft were droning towards the islands of Wake and Guam and the northern Philippines. Urgent messages were speeding between Prime Minister Winston Churchill in London and President Franklin D. Roosevelt in Washington.

Above all, America had already suffered the most humiliating defeat in her history. Her proud Pacific fleet lay beneath the scummy oily waters at Pearl Harbour, in the Hawaiian island of Oahu. In a lightning, daring attack lasting just over two hours, five mighty American battleships had been wrecked, plus four other warships and almost 200 aircraft. More than 2,400 Americans had been slaughtered. And all at a Japanese loss of only 29 aircraft and 55 men. Thick black smoke billowed high above the beautiful island of Oahu, as the Japanese radio announcer gave the news of this stupendous victory to faraway Tokyo. Pearl Harbour itself remained in dreadful turmoil.

Pearl Harbour

11

Winston Churchill goes to the House of Commons to announce the beginning of hostilities with Japan, 1941

Upturned, the battleships' hulks glistened like whale carcasses in the Pacific sunshine.

"In all military history," wrote one Japanese historian describing these attacks on 8th December, "I do not know of any country which simultaneously launched so many battles of such magnitude and, in addition, so completely defeated its opponents as we did on that fateful morning . . . We coordinated our combat operations across a distance of six thousand nautical miles, spanning the ocean between Hawaii and Singapore (1)." Never has any war been opened with such a shattering series of blows. One excited Japanese pilot in the attack on Pearl Harbour felt fully justified in immediately radioing the prearranged victory signal: *Tora! Tora! Tora!"* – "Tiger! Tiger! Tiger!"

Japan's flag, with its huge blood-coloured sun, seemed to fly triumphant over the whole Pacific. And on this 8th December painful questions were already being asked in Washington and London. How could the Japanese attacks have been so successful? Why were the British and Americans taken so much by surprise?

These questions are still asked today. The clues lie many years back in the past, in the decades when Japan, often ignored and isolated, secretly prepared her forces, and when British and American plans and preoccupations were turned elsewhere.

Seeds of tragedy   The seeds of the Pearl Harbour tragedy were sown early in the twentieth century. The major Western powers – Britain, France, America and Germany – were busy with problems in the Western hemisphere, especially during the First World War. With peace in 1918 came hopes of disarmament, and military forces were reduced. Japan's isolation grew. With this isolation went a Japanese policy of expansion, especially at the expense of her traditional enemies, Russia and China. The Western powers paid little heed to Japan's desire to enlarge her territory. Far Eastern affairs took second place.

Hakko Ichiu   At this time, the Japanese began thinking about two fundamental ideas. The first was *Hakko Ichiu* – "bringing the eight corners of the world under one roof." It originated from a saying by the Emperor Jimmu in about 600 B.C., and soon came to represent the spirit of Japanese growth.

The second idea summed up the means for achieving the first: *Bushido*, or "the way of the warrior". The Japanese would win and rule their world according to the ancient samurai, or knightly, code. It was a code of ruthlessness, honour, self-sacrifice, physical endurance and ambition.

General Nogi Maresuke, appointed tutor for Hirohito in 1908, gave the future Emperor a set of rules. They could have applied to Japan herself. Here are some of them: *Education of an Emperor*

"Inquire of your parents about your ancestors, your crest and lineage, and keep them well in mind.

"Be ashamed of torn clothes, but never of patched ones.

"When you order your Western-style clothing, boots, and shoes, have them made larger than your present size, regardless of fashion. You will outgrow them (2)."

The young Hirohito received a spartan education. It included being made to stand naked under an icy waterfall until he learned to control his shivering. Meanwhile Japan pursued her violent and dangerous policies. Formosa had been wrested from China in a war of 1894–95. In 1905 Japan challenged and defeated Russia, against great odds. Five years later she annexed the ancient kingdom of Korea. As a result of the First World War, Japan received a mandate to all former German possessions in the Pacific north of the Equator, which she had already seized as war booty.

By now Japan had emerged as a strong rival to America in the Pacific. Indeed, during the 1920s the two nations were already on a collision course. International attempts at disarmament, especially the British and American insistence upon a naval limitation treaty in 1930, merely allowed Japanese militarists to tell their people that the Americans were trying to keep Japan weak. Meanwhile, China became the main point at issue between Japan and America: Japanese expansion threatened China, and America soon sought to check Tokyo. A liberal Japanese Government agreed to sign a Nine-Power Treaty on 6th February, 1922. The nations agreed "to respect the sovereignty, the independence, and the territorial and admini- *Rivalry with America* strative integrity of China." But hopes raised by this treaty soon faded.

Japan's economy
Japan, like the rest of the world, was hit by the economic disasters of 1929 and 1931. Her population had soared by 20 millions to 70 millions since 1914; industry had flourished. Japan badly needed raw materials and markets for her finished products, yet Britain and other industrial nations imposed barriers against them to try to safeguard their own economies. This quickened Japan's desire to dominate China, which was already her biggest market for cotton, and almost her only source of coal and iron.

Manchukuo annexed
Extremists in Japan received swelling support for their policy of complete control over this invaluable neighbour. In 1931 Japanese troops invaded Manchuria, on the pretext of local disorders, and created the puppet state of Manchukuo in early 1932. China appealed to the League of Nations. The League vainly called on Japan to withdraw her troops, and in 1933 declared that the state of Manchukuo could not be recognized. But Japan's encroachment continued.

Japan's Cabinet had been hand-picked by the Army after a spate of assassinations and murder attempts. On 11th August, 1936, it announced: "The fundamental national policy to be established by the Empire is to secure the position of the Empire on the East Asia Continent by dint of diplomatic policy and national defence, mutually dependent on each other, as well as to advance and develop the Empire toward the South Seas."

German alliance
Soon, it was clear that Japan might expect awesome support. Only three months later, in November, she signed the "Anti-Comintern Pact" with Germany. Ostensibly it was to provide mutual help in the fight against Communism:

"The Government of the German Reich and the Imperial Japanese Government: in recognition of the fact that the aim of the Communist International, called 'Comintern', is the disintegration of . . . existing States with all means at its command . . . Desiring to cooperate for defence against Communist disintegration, have agreed as follows:

"1. . . . To keep one another informed concerning counter-measures, and to carry out the latter in close collaboration.

14

"2. . . . To invite third States whose internal peace is menaced by the disintegrating work of the Communist International to adopt defensive measures in the spirit of the present agreement, or to participate in the present agreement . . . (3)"

And eight months later in July, 1937, Japan launched a full-scale invasion of China, threatened by the Communists – according to Tokyo. The Japanese Prime Minister, Prince Konoye, declared: "In sending troops into North China, of course, the Government has no other purpose . . . than to preserve the peace of East Asia . . . Japan never looks upon the Chinese people as an enemy (4)." *Invasion of China*

America found herself in an awkward position. Her forces were still unprepared for war; nor did many American people support the idea of war. To denounce Japanese aggression would only give the Tokyo Government more support at home. Yet Japan had flagrantly violated the 1922 treaty. In a statement of 17th August, 1937, the American Secretary of State Cordell Hull summed up the dilemma between letting Japan go on unhindered, and over-reacting without adequate military force. America had been caught between two views, he said. "One is the view of extreme internationalism, which rests upon the idea of political commitments. We keep entirely away from that in our thoughts and views and policies, just as we seek, on the other hand, to keep entirely away from the extreme nationalists who would tell all Americans they must stay here at home." *America neutral*

British attention was still fixed on Europe: Hitler seemed about to invade Czechoslovakia. So the West put its trust in the League of Nations, and in an 18-nation meeting called at Brussels. Concerning the latter, President Roosevelt said on the radio on 12th October: *Talks on China*

"The purpose of this conference will be to seek by agreement a solution of the present situation in China. In efforts to find that solution, it is our purpose to cooperate with the other signatories of the [1922] Treaty, including China and Japan."

But Japan refused to take part, and the conference merely proposed a suspension of hostilities and offered to mediate. Japan replied that the China "Incident" was her own affair. America still relied on gentle diplomacy to keep the peace, even

15

Overleaf February, 1938: Chinese troops defending a stretch of frontier against Japanese attack during the Sino-Japanese war

after Japanese aircraft dive-bombed and machine-gunned the U.S. gunboat *Panay* in Chinese waters on 12th December. A Gallup opinion poll held in January, 1938, showed that the mass of Americans wanted complete withdrawal of U.S. ships, missionaries, medical teams and other personnel from threatened China, rather than further involvement.

Japanese demands   So Japan pressed on, heedless of international pressures. On 22nd December, 1938, her Prime Minister announced a list of preposterous demands which would have to be met before peace could be agreed: military operations would seek "the complete extermination" of the Chinese Government, and a "New Order in East Asia" would have to be created. China must accept the "independence" of Manchukuo, submit to Japanese military occupation, and allow an economic protectorate to be formed.

Fierce fighting went on in China throughout 1939. Moreover in July, 1938 and again in May, 1939, undeclared hostilities took place between Japan and Russia over disputed borders. The latter led to Japan renouncing the anti-Comintern Pact with Germany, on 23rd August, 1939, after Hitler had signed the Nazi–Soviet Treaty. But the outbreak of the Second World War in Europe drew Western eyes still further away from Japan, now almost forgotten by many politicians and military leaders in Europe and America. And yet Japan's fight against the stubborn Chinese gave her one great advantage: her forces could be hardened for the war with the West which many Japanese militants were sure would come.

18

2 Rehearsal

JAPAN HAD EXPECTED easy conquest in China. Instead, her troops became bogged down in vicious fighting, unable to force the enemy leader, Chiang Kai-shek, to capitulate. Also, the nationalists had at least the nominal support of the Communist Chinese, with whom they had previously been in bitter conflict. The Communists under Mao Tse-tung were preparing for a highly successful war against the invaders, which they began in 1940. The perceptive Mao steeped his followers in the tactics and strategy of guerrilla warfare.

Mao hits back at Japan

His words had a powerful impact. He told his followers in June, 1939: "The richest sources of power to wage war lies in the masses of the people. It is mainly because of the unorganized state of the Chinese masses that Japan dares to bully us. When this defect is remedied, then the Japanese aggressor, like a mad bull crashing into a ring of flames, will be surrounded by hundreds of millions of our people standing upright, the mere sound of their voices will strike terror into him, and he will be burned to death (5)."

Late in 1939 Japan had to adopt a new strategy of attrition in China. Her campaigns had been inconclusive, and she had found it hard to control a large hostile population. In 1939 the Japanese seized Hainan Island and most of China's seaports, hoping to block foreign supplies to the struggling nationalists. But two doors were still open: the first was the narrow-gauge railway from Haiphong, in French Indochina, to Kumming; the second lay through the harsh country from British Burma – the famous Burma Road. Soon, Japan would press the British

War of attrition

19

hard for the closure of this route, and the dangers of conflict with Britain grew.

Meanwhile, the Second World War opened in Europe with Hitler's forces over-running Poland. Then hostilities dwindled into the "phoney war": British and French troops faced the Germans throughout the winter of 1939–40 with few large-scale clashes, and with the allies still unaware of the many defects in their armies.

The Japanese, on the other hand, were learning from their enemies in China. Despite setbacks and lack of real military progress, they gained valuable experience in the difficult areas of military supply, equipment, command organization, and fighting tactics. Troops learned how to live in rough country on minimum supplies, how to plan and execute those plans with maximum speed. The men who proved themselves in hard combat were quickly promoted. Commanders learned in a real war situation which men and units were most skilful and brave. The same applied to naval and air forces.

Thus, while the British and French troops waited in their sodden trenches for the main fighting to begin in Europe, and while the Americans remained neutral from the conflict, Japanese airmen flew one hazardous mission after another against their courageous foes. This commendation for bravery shows the type of valuable experience gained by the Japanese:

"To the 12th Air Corps Fighter Squadron commanded by Lieutenant Saburo Shindo: On 13th September, 1940, this squadron made a successful long-range flight over the mountainous Ssuchuan-Sheng area, escorting the Chungking bombing expedition of the land-based attack bomber group. After completing their escort mission and appearing to leave the target area for the purpose of luring enemy fighters from hiding, the squadron returned to Chungking to attack a numerically superior enemy fighter force, succeeding in destroying all the enemy fighters through gallant and courageous combat. This outstanding success deserves the Distinguished Military Merit. I hereby award this Diploma of Merit. Shigetaro Shimada. Commander-in-Chief, China Area Fleet (6)."

Life proved hard for these young Japanese, and not only in

actual fighting. Non-combat training was made as stiff as possible. Navy pilots, selected from sub-lieutenants and ensigns, had a year's preliminary flight training, but they had to spend at least another year in training before qualifying as aircraft carrier pilots and forward fighting area pilots. "We maintained the strictest requirements for these young men," wrote one Japanese, "for, despite their age, they were responsible for the operation of elaborate and expensive machines and apparatus of which Japan was continually in short supply (7)."

Even normal exercises were exacting and dangerous. In routine navy manoeuvres up to 100 men might be lost overboard in high seas or killed by operational accidents. A Japanese Navy Department pamphlet stated:

Casualties in training

"In recent years, the activities of the Fleet have been as follows. Leaving home ports the latter part of January and carrying out intensive training for the greater part of the year in the stormy Pacific or in out-of-the way gulfs where human habitations are extremely scarce, with hardly a day of rest other than two or three days at anchor for recreation after . . . sometimes more than a month of operating . . . There are no Saturdays or Sundays, especially when under way, where one drill follows another – literally a period of no sleep. This is because if we are not under way we cannot carry out actual battle training, and so with a tenacious and tireless spirit we are striving to reach a superhuman degree of skill and perfect fighting efficiency (8)."

The men were not alone in receiving stern testing. Equipment and weapons, too, were improved as a result of tough experience, including aircraft of the type later used against the U.S. Pacific Fleet. Admiral Toyota, Chief of the Japanese Navy Aeronautics Bureau, sent this signal on 14th September, 1940:

Aircraft

"To: Mr. Koshiro Shiba, Chairman, Board of Directors, Mitsubishi Heavy Industry Company, Ltd. The recent outstanding success of the 12th Air Corps Zero fighter squadron in attacking and destroying 27 Chinese fighters over Chungking on 13th September, 1940, without loss to themselves, is due in great part to the excellent performance of the Zero fighter. I hereby express my sincere gratitude, and the gratitude of the

Overleaf Japanese sailors wearing gas-masks during the rigorous naval exercises carried out by the Japanese navy before the Second World War. One of the few contemporary pictures published in the West.

Navy, for the outstanding and meritorious work of your company in completing within a short development time this excellent fighter (9)."

Carriers for attack

As the Japanese improved their training, fighting efficiency, weapons and equipment, they also gave careful study to large-scale plans for future war. In 1937 both American and Japanese naval doctrines laid down that aircraft carriers should primarily be used to provide air cover for a striking force of battleships. Next year, this idea underwent radical change in Japan. Aircraft, especially bombers, were seen as growing in importance. Massive battleships had only proved of limited value in the First World War, and had since been made vulnerable through air power.

So, in 1938, the Japanese adopted the idea that aircraft carriers should be used as a weapon in their own right – as bases for launching attacks deep into enemy territory, or across wide expanses of sea at the enemy fleet, thus emphasizing the advantages of mobility and surprise. Ironically, it was probably the Americans who first showed the Japanese how important these vessels were. Admiral Nagano, Chief of the Japanese Naval General Staff, admitted: "Our principal teacher in respect to the necessity of emphasizing aircraft carriers was the American Navy. We had no teachers to speak of besides the United States in respect to the aircraft themselves (10)."

Ten new aircraft carriers

Japan began building 30,000-ton 30-knot carriers, and experimenting with suitable aircraft to operate from them. By the time of Pearl Harbour she would have ten of these vessels in commission; the U.S. Navy, on the other hand, would only have five – three of them in the Pacific.

A Japanese historian wrote in 1941: "We intensified our training programme, concentrating on those tactics most likely to be needed in a war of major scope. The long combat missions in China proved of immense value in reforming our front-line groups . . . By late November of 1941, with the special three months' period of intensive training completed, all the Navy's air units were fully prepared for battle, confident in their men, their machines, and their ground-support groups."

This confidence is shown in the excitement of a Japanese

seaman, Kuramoto, when told of the plan to attack Pearl Harbour: "An air attack on Hawaii! A dream come true. What will the people at home think when they hear the news? Won't they be excited! I can see them clapping their hands and shouting with joy! We would teach the Anglo-Saxon scoundrels a lesson!"

During this late period many American experts vastly *American* underrated Japanese military efficiency. An article in the U.S. *ignorance* magazine *Aviation*, published only three months before Pearl Harbour, declared: "America's aviation experts can say without hesitation that the chief military airplanes of Japan are either outdated already, or are becoming outdated . . ."

The Japanese, with their secret preparations, knew better. Armed by experience and supreme self-confidence, pilots only waited for the politicians to finish talking and order the attack.

These plans had been veiled in strict security. Even the war *Security* in China had been fought behind the scenes, while the spotlight had turned to great events elsewhere. These were the years and months of the fall of France, the desperate struggle waged by Britain to ward off German invasion, the grim conflict between U-boats and merchantmen in the grey Atlantic, the see-saw campaigns against Erich Rommel, the legendary "Desert Fox," in the scorching sands of North Africa, and, eventually, the German–Soviet struggle in the frozen wastes of Russia.

Threats from Japan had to be put in second place. And yet *The leaders* the subject of Japan grew almost daily in importance to baffle the minds of the Western leaders – Franklin Roosevelt, taciturn, sometimes evasive, anxious to enter the world struggle but hampered by domestic desires for peace; Winston Churchill, ebullient, magnificent in his defiance of Hitler when Britain stood alone, yet insistent that Japan could be deterred.

In Tokyo, the Government gradually moved closer to war, although not without doubts. Matsuoka, Foreign Minister until July, 1941, wavered between a desire for moderation and anger at the stubborn Americans. Another moderate, Prime Minister Prince Konoye, found himself replaced by the sinister and militant War Minister, Tojo Hideki. Above them all ruled the aloof, elusive and impenetrable Emperor Hirohito.

25

Overleaf Heavy Japanese warships carrying out manoeuvres off the coast of China – a prelude to hostilities against America and Britain

Cordell Hull, U.S. Secretary of State, gives the nation news of the
negotiations with Japan

3 Diplomatic Chessboard

DIPLOMATS of many nations worked to avert war. When this became impossible, they schemed to gain time and choose the best moment to strike. And behind their discussions were those of the military planners. How and where should their forces be deployed? Should the bulk of American naval forces be in the Pacific or Atlantic? Which area faced the greatest threat? Which targets were most likely to be attacked?

The diplomats

Top-level talks continued throughout these tense months of 1940 and 1941 in Washington, London and Tokyo. President Roosevelt spoke with his advisers in the elegant White House, where the outwardly peaceful atmosphere made grim war seem far away. In London, Winston Churchill's War Cabinet met at 10 Downing Street, or, when German bombers battered the British capital, in the austere, green-painted underground War Room, deep below Whitehall.

Talks (1940—41)

Japanese meetings were in sharp contrast to Roosevelt's informal gatherings, and Churchill's well-conducted and orderly Cabinet sessions. Tokyo held "Liaison Conferences", attended both by politicians and senior military men. They were described by a Japanese official:

Japan's Liaison Conferences

"Liaison Conferences were held in a smaller conference room, and around the conference room were armchairs. Somewhat in the centre along the farther end of the room sat the Prime Minister and a circle was formed around him ... Liaison Conferences were held between the representatives of the Government and of the High Command, to bring about a meeting of minds between the two on various issues. . . . There was no presiding officer, and every member spoke freely. And therefore at times two men would start talking at the same time, or one member would be whispering to another while another was speaking. Secretaries were constantly leaving and entering the room . . . (11)"

Meetings often erupted into a hubbub of raised voices, argument and angry interruptions. Final Japanese decisions were ratified at an Imperial Conference, attended by the Emperor himself, who sat in front of a gold screen.

America: how neutral? America's position was made difficult by her neutral role. Until she entered the war she had to avoid being branded an aggressor. Plans for war had to be cautious. A sudden entry into war could be disastrous, both because the American people wanted peace to last as long as possible, and above all because she had still to build up military strength. Her weapons, manpower and other military resources were severely limited. She had too little power to plan for both full-scale war in the West – Europe and the Atlantic area – and in the Pacific. One or the other had to be chosen as the main area of war. But which was it to be?

"Rainbow Two" When war broke out between the European powers in September, 1939, the neutral Americans still based plans on the so-called "Rainbow Two" scheme. This assumed that, when the country eventually entered the fighting, "the United States, Great Britain and France would be acting in concert, with limited participation of U.S. forces in continental Europe and in the Atlantic. The United States could, therefore, undertake immediate offensive operations across the Pacific (12)." This scheme assumed that Britain and France would be strong enough to deal with the enemy in Europe, with only minimum American help; the main American offensive effort would be in the Far East.

Crisis in Europe Suddenly, in May 1940, the "phoney war" ended in Europe, as Hitler launched his *blitzkrieg* against the British and French Within days the Allied armies had been thrown off-balance and were sent tumbling back. Denmark and Norway had been occupied in April. At the end of May the retreating British Army had to be rescued from the Dunkirk beaches. On 10th June, Italy

30

entered the war on the German side. France seemed on the verge of total collapse; Britain suddenly stood alone and wide open to invasion.

"Rainbow Two" scrapped

This disaster called for an urgent revision of the American plans: "Rainbow Two" was now out of date. Britain and France were going to need all possible American help, diverted from the Pacific. On 13th June, President Roosevelt called for an evaluation of the situation. His planners saw three main choices: "*1* To maintain a strong position in the Pacific, and to avoid commitment everywhere else. *2* To make every effort, including belligerent participation, to sustain Great Britain and France. *3* To take whatever measures were required to prevent Axis penetration into the Western Hemisphere (i.e. American territory) (13)."

The first choice would mean virtually abandoning Britain and France to their fate; the second would mean giving up the Pacific and closing down bases such as Pearl Harbour.

Today, it is easy to criticize the American government for even thinking of abandoning the British and French to Hitler. But in those grim days things looked very different. By the time help came it might be too late: the slender American forces which would soon be needed for home defence might be wasted and lost.

One sign of how desperate things were is given by the many references to the British fleet during this period. The Americans believed total British defeat to be so near that they feared for their own safety should the powerful Royal Navy fall into German hands.

If Hitler takes the Royal Navy

Churchill himself fed these fears, which seemed perfectly justifiable. He cabled Roosevelt on 15th June: "Although the present government and I personally would never fail to send the Fleet across the Atlantic if resistance was beaten down here, a point may be reached in the struggle where the present Ministers no longer have control of affairs ... The fate of the British Fleet ... would be decisive on the future of the United States, because if it were joined to the Fleets of Japan, France (under German control), and Italy and the great resources of German industry, overwhelming sea-power would be in Hitler's

Overleaf U.S. battleship *Arizona* destroyed with her crew of eleven hundred during the attack on Pearl Harbour

hands . . . (14)"

American isolationism

In view of this grim warning, top American planners insisted that American defence should come first. On 17th June, 1940, General George Strong, Chief of the War Plans Division, asked that all available resources should be brought back from the Pacific; nothing more should be done to help Britain. Strong admitted that he expected "the early defeat of the Allies, an admission of our inability to furnish means in quantities sufficient to affect the situation, and an acknowledgment that we recognize the probability that we are next on the list of Axis powers (15)."

Hitler's victories aid Japan

In fact, Hitler's conquest of France and the Low Countries opened the way for Japanese encroachment in the Far East – France and Holland had extensive possessions in the area. With the fall of France, Japan demanded permission to send a "military mission" into French Indo-China. On 20th June the defeated French agreed. In the same month, Japan threatened Britain with war unless British troops were shipped out of Shanghai, and the border between Hong Kong and China was blocked. Japan clearly meant to use the situation to try to cut China off from the outside world.

America's Defence Act (1940)

America was virtually powerless. All she could do was to use diplomatic and commercial pressure. The National Defense Act, passed in May, allowed the President to keep all products at home that might be needed for defence, including oil: "Whenever the President determines that it is necessary in the interest of national defense to prohibit or curtail the exportation of any military equipment or munitions . . . or materials . . . he may by proclamation prohibit or curtail such exportation (16)."

Churchill's warning

Such measures were unlikely to deter Tokyo. Strong military action was needed to block Japanese advances, and yet America's fears for her own safety persisted. At any moment Britain might be invaded. "The whole fury and might of the enemy must very soon be turned on us," warned Churchill in the House of Commons on 18th June. And he added: "If we fail, then the whole world including the United States, including all that we have known and cared for, will sink into the abyss of a new Dark Age (17)."

In America, experts anxiously asked that the British Fleet should sail across the Atlantic rather than fall into German hands, and added that ammunition and material should perhaps be sent now in readiness. Churchill sent a stern reply on 22nd June: "There is no warrant for such precautions at the present time (18)." Roosevelt still wanted a public assurance that if the war went badly the Fleet would leave British waters to fight overseas. Churchill replied in haughty tones on 7th August: "Our position is not such as to bring the collapse of Britain into the arena of practical discussion." *Fears for the fleet*

Fortunately, Churchill proved correct. Hitler postponed his plans to invade England, and instead threw his air force against the R.A.F. in the Battle of Britain. The brave British pilots broke the Luftwaffe sword.

American observers came to Britain in August, including General Strong. They were struck by Britain's coolness and determination. She might yet survive – if American help were given. Staff officers in London said that "we [the British] were certainly relying on the continued economic and industrial cooperation of the United States in ever increasing volume," and supplies were "fundamental to our whole strategy (19)." *America: Britain has a chance*

Meanwhile, the Japanese military leaders were demanding bolder action in the Far East. On 27th July, 1940, the Japanese Cabinet decided "to maintain a firm attitude towards America on the one hand . . . to take stronger measures against French Indo-China, Hong Kong and foreign concessions in China looking to the prevention of aid to the Chiang regime . . . To practise more vigorous diplomacy towards the Netherlands East Indies, in order to acquire vital materials . . . (20)" *Japanese boldness*

On 4th September the scope of Japanese expansion hopes was made clear to all in an awesome policy document: "Japan's Sphere of Living for the construction of a Greater East Asia New Order will comprise: the former German Islands under mandate, French Indochina and Pacific Islands, Thailand, British Malaya, British Borneo, Dutch East Indies, Burma, Australia, New Zealand, India, etc., with Japan, Manchuria and China as the backbone (21)." *Japan debates pact with*

Japan, Germany and Italy were clearly moving closer together, *Hitler* 35 and in September their talks were directed toward a full-scale alliance. On 19th September, 1940, the Imperial Conference met in Tokyo to consider such a treaty. Notes taken at this meeting show how the Japanese were thinking:

Army Chief of Staff Prince Kan'in: "What effect would closer cooperation between Japan, Germany and Italy have on the settlement of the China Incident?"

Foreign Minister Matsuoka: "In order to strengthen and improve Japan's position in negotiating this Pact, we have informed Germany that Japan would settle the China Incident through her own efforts. However, we hope to receive help from Germany after the conclusion of the Pact . . . I believe we can anticipate considerable results . . . "

Navy Chief of Staff Prince Fushimi: "I foresee that as a result of this alliance our trade with Great Britain and the United States will undergo a change; and that if worst come to worst, it will become increasingly difficult to import vital materials. . ."

Prime Minister Konoye: "Trade relations with Britain and the United States will deteriorate even more . . . It may become impossible to obtain any imported goods. . . Our country depends to a large extent on Britain and the United States for her principal war materials. . ."

President of the Privy Council Hara: "I should like to add that this Pact is a treaty of alliance with the United States as its target . . . When Japan's position becomes clear with the announcement of this Pact, she [America] will greatly increase her pressure on us, she will greatly step up her aid to Chiang, and she will obstruct Japan's war effort . . . She will attempt to weaken us over the long term so that we will not be able to endure war."

The Japanese leaders were still showing caution. Full war preparations had still to be completed. The position was summed up by Hara, President of the Privy Council, on behalf of the Emperor: "Even though a Japanese–American clash may be unavoidable in the end, I hope that sufficient care will be exercised to make sure that it will not come in the near future, and that there will be no miscalculations. I give my approval on this basis (22)."

And so Japan, Germany and Italy put their signatures to the Tripartite Pact on 27th September. They promised "to assist one another with all political, economic and military means when one of the three Contracting Parties is attacked by a power at present not involved in the European War, or in the Sino-Japanese conflict."

America, as the Japanese had intended, was clearly the target. British Cabinet Ministers agreed that "the Pact, which would probably anger the United States, left matters very much as they were, and did not affect the general situation. If anything, it was likely to accelerate the entry of the United States into the war (23)."

Only five days before the Pact was signed, Japanese troops had overrun northern French Indochina. Both moves – the alliance and the renewed aggression – increased American difficulties. On 25th September, 48 hours before the Pact was signed, U.S. army planners had finished a study on how best to deal with the multiple threats both in the West and in the Pacific. The experts felt that since the greater danger lay in the Atlantic, operations in the Pacific should be kept to the minimum. This view was accepted.

They believed that Japan would not attack American or British possessions in the Far East until German victory seemed certain in Europe. All help must be given to Britain in the Atlantic area, at the expense of a proper defence in the Far East and Pacific.

America must face Hitler

Discussions continued on this daring policy. It even led to the turning down of British pleas for help in the Far East. As Cordell Hull, U.S. Secretary of State, told the British Ambassador: "It will not be wise, even from the British standpoint, for two wars to be raging at the same time, one in the East and the other in the West. If this country should enter any war, this would immediately result in greatly cutting off military supplies to Great Britain (24)."

This emphasis on the West instead of the Pacific now led to a concrete American plan, first revealed to the British War Cabinet on 6th November. "The review of present situation was gloomy," reported the British Naval Attaché in Washington.

America's plan

39

Confident allies: the Japanese Foreign Minister Matsuoka with the German leader Ribbentrop, during negotiations for their Tripartite Pact in 1940

"Conclusion reached was that British programme – without considerable competent aid from American navy – was impossible. Appreciation anticipated ultimate completion of Axis [Germany and Italy] control in Mediterranean, and argued that this would largely nullify British blockade. Argument followed that very considerable direct naval, military and air assistance in European area must be given to the British to ensure victory... A fully offensive war by the U.S. against Japan would involve the whole of American naval and industrial resources and . . . the U.S. Navy would be unable to provide the minimum of assistance in the Atlantic and Europe necessary to prevent a British defeat (25)."

This appreciation marked a complete reversal of U.S. plans made before Hitler's conquest of France. These plans, especially "Rainbow Two", had envisaged limited American aid in the West and an *offensive* campaign against Japan in the event of war. Now the Americans favoured maximum help to Britain and a *defensive* stand in the Far East against Japan. Inevitably, this increased the dangers from a Japanese surprise attack.

"Plan Dog"
Admiral Stark duly submitted his appreciation to President Roosevelt in November. It became known as Plan Dog because of the crucial paragraph D (D for "Dog" in military code). This urged the President to "direct our efforts towards an eventual strong offensive in the Atlantic as an ally of the British, and a defensive in the Pacific (26)." Roosevelt approved the scheme, which was put into effect on 16th January, 1941.

Meanwhile, President Roosevelt had also been pondering the overall question of aid to Britain. He knew that America's capacity to help was still very limited. Also, she was still officially neutral. Still, he wanted to make it as easy as possible for Britain to obtain goods from America.

Roosevelt: help Britain
On 17th December, Roosevelt told a press conference: "The best immediate defence of the United States is the success of Great Britain. . . What I am trying to do is to eliminate the dollar sign. This is something brand new in the thoughts of practically everybody in this room, I think. Get rid of the silly, foolish dollar sign."

On 29th December he added: "The British people are conducting an active war against the unholy alliance. . . Our own future security is greatly dependent on the outcome . . . I make the direct statement to the American people that there is a far less chance of the United States getting into the war if we do all we can now to support the nations defending themselves against attack." Britain must have the tools of war "in sufficient volume and quickly enough so that we and our children will be saved the agony and suffering of war."

Winston Churchill told the British War Cabinet next day that "although President Roosevelt's speech of the previous day had been in general terms, it had been satisfactory from our point of view, and he had been encouraged by it. It committed the U.S. to implacable hostility and resistance (27)."

From Roosevelt's policy emerged the "Lend-Lease" Bill, which became law on Tuesday, 11th March, 1941. It authorized the President to "sell, transfer title to, exchange, lease, lend or otherwise dispose of . . . any defense article" to any nation whose defence he deemed vital to U.S. security.

"Lend-Lease" (March, 1941)

At the same time joint Anglo-American staff talks opened in Washington to discuss military planning. The British began by stating their position:

Joint talks

"1. The European theatre is the vital theatre where a decision must first be sought.

"2. The general policy should therefore be to defeat Germany and Italy first, and then to deal with Japan." And yet the statement continued:

"3. The security of the Far Eastern position, including Australia and New Zealand, is essential to the cohesion of the British Commonwealth and to the maintenance of its war effort. Singapore is the key to the defence of these interests and its retention must be assured (28)."

So the problem still had to be solved. Although most emphasis was to be placed in the Western area of war, vital interests in the Far East still had to be protected. But with what forces, when all were needed in the Atlantic area? The Anglo-American planners completed their work in March and handed in their report on the 27th. This study, titled *ABC-1*, declared:

"The Atlantic and European area is considered to be the

Policy fixed 41

Overleaf President Roosevelt signs the "Lend-Lease" Bill – a bill designed to help strengthen the defences of America's allies

decisive theatre . . . If Japan does enter the war, the military strategy in the Far East will be defensive. The United States does not intend to add to its present military strength in the Far East, but will employ the United States Pacific Fleet offensively in the manner best calculated to weaken Japanese economic power, and to support the defense of the Malay barrier by diverting Japanese strength away from Malaysia (29)."

Risks

Thus the official Anglo-American policy had been decided. Terrible risks had to be taken. Far East interests were seen as vital, yet American strength in the area would not be increased. No offensive plans were made. This left the Japanese the great advantage of choosing their own time and direction for attack.

Hitler: Japan must act

Already, the Germans had put pressure on the Japanese for an early offensive: Hitler stated on 5th March: "It must be the aim of the collaboration based on the Three Power Pact to induce Japan as soon as possible to take active measures in the Far East . . . The seizure of Singapore . . . would mean a decisive success for the entire conduct of the war of the Three Powers. In addition, attacks on other systems of bases of British naval power – extending to those of American naval power only if entry of the United States into the war cannot be prevented – will result in the weakening of the enemy's system of power in that region (30)."

Allied complacency

And yet, despite the risks of concentrating on the West, a complacency existed in Washington and London. General Marshall, Chief of the American Staff, wrote a memorandum to President Roosevelt in May, 1941, which soon proved deplorably incorrect. It concerned the Island of Oahu and its naval base, Pearl Harbour. General Marshall wrote: "Due to its fortification, its garrison and its physical characteristics, Pearl Harbour is believed to be the strongest fortress in the world . . . With adequate air defense, enemy carriers, naval escorts and transports will begin to come under air attack at a distance of approximately 750 miles. This attack will increase in intensity until within 200 miles of the objective the enemy forces will be subject to attack by all types of bombardment closely supported by our most modern pursuit . . . With this force available a major attack against Oahu is considered impracticable (31)."

The British War Cabinet also underestimated Japanese ability and determination. Early in January, Ministers agreed with Churchill that "the defeats, particularly the naval defeats, which we had inflicted upon the Italians, would strongly influence the Japanese. The mistake of taking warships at their paper-value had been brought home to them (32)."

The main defeat referred to by Churchill was that suffered by the Italians at Taranto, following the lightning attack by aircraft from the carrier *Illustrious* the previous November. Yet this British success, rather than deterring the Japanese, encouraged them to think along the same lines. And as for the British Prime Minister's mocking reference to "paper-value", total allied naval presence in the Far East during these increasingly dangerous months of 1941, remained terribly small.

Europe still claimed priority.

4 Summer Tightrope

War scares

SUDDEN SCARES of war in the Far East began to disturb the planners in Washington and London. These alarms grew more frequent during spring and summer, 1941. As early as 6th February the British War Cabinet met to discuss some disquieting news about Japan. The Foreign Secretary, Anthony Eden, revealed that on the previous day Japan had warned her Embassy staff in London "to reduce their contacts with the British authorities to a minimum and to be prepared to leave the country at short notice." The British Joint Intelligence Sub-Committee warned that a Japanese assault on the Dutch East Indies was on the cards. The Chiefs of Staff told the Cabinet that Britain could do nothing in the Far East; all possible reinforcements had already been sent, and Britain and America should instead rely upon a firm diplomatic stand.

The British Embassy told the U.S. State Department on the 7th February: "Evidence is accumulating that the Japanese may already have decided to push on southward, even if this means war." And on 15th February, Churchill warned Roosevelt: "The weight of the Japanese Navy, if thrown against us, would confront us with situations beyond the scope of our naval resources (33)."

Code-breakers

This scare soon subsided, but tension remained. Close watch was kept upon Japanese movements; agents sent in a flow of reports; Japanese radio signals were constantly monitored. Here the Americans scored a dramatic success. Experts managed to crack the Japanese codes and secret cyphers known as "Magic." This enabled the Americans to read top-level messages between Tokyo and overseas Ambassadors; they could study

47

The Japanese advance in Malaya. Armoured vehicles with specially adapted wheels use the railways in the drive into the heart of British-held territory reports sent by military *attachés* and agents, and enjoy the big advantage of knowing the instructions being sent out by the Japanese Government.

But there was one major drawback. War scares multiplied, because the secret messages often seemed to point to imminent Japanese military action. And as war scares multiplied they decreased in impact: they became almost commonplace. Thus, when the Pearl Harbour attack was imminent, the evidence about it was easily overlooked. After all, similar information had appeared before, without war actually breaking out.

Russo-German alliance In late spring a new factor confused things still further: Germany moved nearer war with Russia. The Japanese Foreign Minister had recently signed a treaty with Russia, her traditional foe. Yet she also had a treaty with Germany. A German–Soviet war would let her join in this strike against the Soviets in the north, or to take advantage of the confusion and strike in the south.

Foreign Minister Matsuoka returned to Tokyo on 22nd April after his visit to Moscow and Berlin. He at once told the Liaison Conference about his talks with the Nazi Foreign Minister, Ribbentrop. Ribbentrop had declared that "Germany would somehow or other like to defeat the Soviet Union. At present we can probably defeat her in three or four months. I think the Soviet Union would disintegrate if she were defeated. If Japan were to attempt a conquest of Singapore, she would no longer need to worry about the North (34)."

Atlantic build-up New opportunities might therefore soon open up for Japan. Yet America, rather than raising her Pacific strength, considered a further reduction in order to build up the Atlantic force.

Churchill was in favour. This "would be of great psychological importance, as well as dealing German naval forces in the Atlantic a decisive blow in the event of hostilities." But the First Sea Lord, Admiral Sir Dudley Pound, argued that such a large fleet would not help the Battle of the Atlantic; it would be better as a deterrent against the Japanese. Eventually Britain replied that she would welcome a larger U.S. naval presence in the Atlantic, but hoped at least six capital ships and two carriers would remain in the Pacific. As a result, three American battleships and a carrier passed into the Atlantic in June; and an ill-fated fleet of nine battleships and three carriers remained based at Pearl Harbour (35).

This debate showed the difficult balance between finding forces for the Atlantic and Pacific – and underlined the fragile strength in the latter. But in Tokyo Foreign Minister Matsuoka still pleaded for more time. He told the Liaison Conference on 8th May: *Arguments in Tokyo*

"America's actions to date are certainly tantamount to participation in the war. I think that Japan, as a great power, should protest them. We know what is happening, but are pretending to be unaware of it. So far Hitler has put up with it, but he might unexpectedly go to war with the United States. I think it might be argued that if this happens, Japan, as a treaty partner, should also go to war. However, from the diplomatic standpoint it's not so easy to do that. It is my intention to prevent the United States from entering the war, and to make her withdraw from China. So please don't rush me . . ."

Navy Minister Oikawa: "The Foreign Minister keeps talking about American participation in the war, but does the U.S. have anything to gain from participation? I think she has much to lose . . . Any further aid to Britain would only be a loss. Although Roosevelt, because of circumstances, is acting as if he were going to jump into the war, I think that now is the most likely time for the United States to make a major change in her national policy."

Matsuoka: "Roosevelt is ready to start a war. He is, after all, a big gambler . . . (36)"

The Japanese leaders were in real confusion during the sultry summer months of 1941. Broadly, the politicians and diplomats argued caution, while the military made loud demands for earlier action. The result was an indecisive, yet dangerous, succession of conferences.

Under German pressure Foreign Minister Matsuoka adopted a more threatening attitude toward America. America, on the other hand, put further restrictions on materials exported to Japan. Matsuoka revealed his tougher line at a meeting of the Liaison Conference on 22nd May: *Japanese threats*

The still of Pearl Harbour

"It now seems inevitable that we must begin an economic war with Britain and the United States . . . They may eventually embargo even tin and rubber. It seems that they are taking advantage of Japan's plight and treating us as a minor power . . . At two o'clock this afternoon I am going to summon the British Ambassador [Sir Robert Craigie] and ask him to tell his Government that the Imperial Government will be forced to resort to armed measures in the South [against the Dutch East Indies] if the present situation continues (37)." But another member pointed out that operations against the East Indies, to obtain the valuable supplies of oil and tin in the islands, would mean operations against Thailand and Indochina to obtain the necessary bases. The subject was deferred to allow more consideration.

Discussion continued on 11th June. Negotiations with the Netherlands East Indies for raw materials had broken down. Matsuoka told the Liaison Conference: "If we are to send troops in, we shall have to do so not only in Indochina but also in Thailand. The deployment of our forces in Indochina and Thailand would necessarily affect Burma and Malaya, and Britain would inevitably get involved."

Army Chief of Staff Sugiyama: "If we are strong, I believe the other side will refrain from action . . . (38) "

But Matsuoka still hesitated to take drastic steps. He told the Liaison Conference on 16th June: "My feeling is that the occupation [of southern Indochina] will unavoidably discredit us internationally. We must remember that Japan has been said to lack integrity in international relations. Another reason the occupation needs to be reconsidered is that Russo-German relations are strained at present. I would like to study this matter." Tojo, the militant War Minister, exclaimed: "If we don't finish the job before the end of the year, we will have to abandon our policy of establishing the Greater East Asia Co-prosperity Sphere." Sugiyama added: "I would like to see blitzkrieg diplomacy (39)."

Suddenly, on 22nd June, 1941, Germany invaded Russia. Hitler's terrible "Barbarossa" campaign had begun. The offensive further complicated talks in Tokyo, and wrangling at the Liaison Conferences grew worse. President Roosevelt guessed that the Japanese were having "a real drag-down and knockout fight . . . to decide which way they are going to jump – attack Russia, attack the South Seas . . . sit on the fence and be more friendly with us (40)."

On 25th June the Liaison Conference agreed that Japan would not be willing after all to risk a war with Britain and America. But this agreement failed to clear the air. Oikawa, the Navy Minister, declared: "You shouldn't talk about the distant future without consulting the Supreme Command. The Navy is confident about a war against the United States and Britain, but not confident about a war against the United States, Britain and the Soviet Union. Suppose the Soviets and the Americans get together, and the United States builds naval bases, air bases, radar stations, etc., on Soviet soil . . . In order to avoid a situation of this kind, don't tell us to strike at Soviet Russia and also tell us to go south. The Navy doesn't want the Soviet Union stirred up."

Matsuoka: "You say you are not afraid of a war with the United States and Britain. So why do you not wish to see the Soviets enter the war?"

Oikawa: "If the Soviets come in, it means fighting an additional country, doesn't it? (41)"

So the Japanese Navy opposed a war with Russia, while Foreign Minister Matsuoka supported it. The Army also wanted to advance north, but was still worried by the stubborn Chinese. *Japanese compromise plan* The Navy and Army managed to draft a compromise plan, discussed by the Liaison Conference on 26th June, which revolved round a "wait and see" policy. The paper declared "Our Empire will continue its efforts to effect a settlement of the China Incident, and will seek to establish a solid basis for the security and preservation of the nation. This will involve taking steps to advance to the South and, furthermore, a settlement of the Northern Question, depending on changes in the situation."

After much argument, Matsuoka finally declared: "I have some basic reservations about the Army–Navy draft, but in the main I agree with it." Muto, Chief of the Military Affairs

Bureau, immediately commented: "If that is the case, please put your agreement in writing." Matsuoka retorted: "I won't put it in writing (42)."

Matsuoka still pressed for an attack on Russia rather than an occupation of southern Indo-China. The first would not bring American intervention, he claimed, while the latter would. "I am not speaking from desperation," he told the Liaison Conference on 27th June. "If we go to war against Soviet Russia, I am confident that I can hold down the United States by diplomacy for three of four months. If we wait and see how the trend goes, as proposed in the draft by the Supreme Command, we will be surrounded by Britain, the United States and Russia. We should first strike north, and then strike south. Nothing ventured, nothing gained (43)."

The military leaders replied that an attack against Russia would take too long to prepare; a strike south should be made first. At last a compromise plan was reached, although biased in favour of the military. It marked a major step towards Pearl Harbour, now only five months away. Preparations began for moves against Malaya, the East Indies, Borneo, the Philippines – and the Hawaian island of Oahu.

Detailed The plan, approved by the Imperial Conference on 2nd July,
plans declared: "Preparations for war with Great Britain and the United States will be made . . . Various measures relating to French Indochina and Thailand will be taken, to strengthen our advance into the southern regions . . ."

As a sop to Matsuoka, the plan continued: "We will secretly strengthen our military preparedness *vis-à-vis* the Soviet Union, and we will deal with this matter independently. In the meantime, we will conduct diplomatic negotiations with great care. If the German–Soviet war should develop to the advantage of our Empire, we will, by resorting to armed force, settle the Northern Question and assure the security of the northern borders. . .

"We will strive to the utmost, by diplomatic and other means, to prevent the entry of the United States into the European war. But if the United States should enter the war, our Empire will act in accordance with the Tripartite Pact. However, we will decide independently as to the time and method of resorting to force.

"We will immediately turn our attention to putting the nation on a war footing ... Concrete plans covering this programme will be drawn up separately (44)."

Diplomatic manoeuvrings intensified. On 21st June U.S. Secretary of State Cordell Hull had handed a Note to the Japanese Ambassador in Washington. Nomura. In it America put her terms for agreement with the Japanese over China, economic matters, the European war, and Pacific affairs. These were all unacceptable to the Japanese.

Even more unacceptable was the content of an "Oral Statement" handed to Nomura by Hull at the same time. This declared that although the Ambassador himself desired peace, the Americans believed that "some Japanese leaders in influential positions" were committed to Nazi Germany. "So long as such leaders maintain this attitude . . . is it not illusory to expect that adoption of a proposal such as the one under consideration offers a basis for achieving substantial results along the desired lines? (45)"

The Japanese Liaison Conference discussed the U.S. Note and the Oral Statement on 10th July. "Hull's statement is outrageous," stormed Matsuoka. "Never has such a thing occurred since Japan opened diplomatic relations with other countries. Ambassador Nomura and I are good friends, but it is inexcusable for him to transmit such an outrageous statement. I was truly amazed that he would listen without protest to a demand that Japan, a great world power, change her Cabinet (46)."

Two days later Matsuoka's anger erupted again at another Liaison Conference session. "It is characteristic of Americans to be high-handed towards the weak. The statement considers Japan a weak, dependent country . . . The United States thinks that Japan is exhausted, and for that reason it sent the statement. I propose here and now that we reject this statement, and that we end negotiations with the United States."

This drastic idea sent even the generals into a shocked silence. Then the Army Chief of Staff, Sugiyama, commented: "I myself agree with the Foreign Minister's views. However, we among

55

Clark Grew, the U.S. Ambassador to Japan with Teijiro Toyoda, who
replaced the diplomat Matsuoka as Japan's Foreign Minister

the military believe it is appropriate on this occasion to leave room for negotiations. It is not yet suitable to tell the United States that we might cut off diplomatic relations, since in the near future we plan to move troops into French Indochina, and since in the North we are directly faced with the grave necessity of strengthening the Kwantung [China] Army."

Matsuoka: "I believe that the American attitude will not change, no matter what attitude Japan takes. It is the nature of American people to take advantage of you if you show weakness . . . (47) "

Japanese brinkmanship

The wrangle ended with a Cabinet reshuffle. Matsuoka found himself replaced by Admiral Toyoda, and the talks went on in Washington. The Japanese were playing a game of brinkmanship. Nagano, Navy Chief of Staff, told his colleagues on 24th July: "As for war with the United States, although there is now a chance of achieving victory, the chances will diminish as time goes on. By the latter half of next year it will already be difficult for us to cope with the United States. After that the situation will become increasingly worse. The United States will probably prolong the matter until her defences have been built up, and then try to settle it (48)."

Armies on the move

Japanese troops began to move into southern Indochina. Since breaking the Japanese diplomatic code, America had already decided upon retaliatory measures: on the evening of 25th July all Japanese assets in the United States were frozen. Trade between the two countries was halted. This was followed on 1st August by an embargo on oil exports to Japan.

Ambassador Nomura cabled from Washington on 7th August: "U.S.–Japanese relations have now reached an extremely critical stage (49)." The Japanese Press Secretary, Ishii Ko, claimed that Japan was being encircled by the "A.B.C.D." powers – American, British, Chinese and Dutch.

Britain: cool the crisis

The new crisis led to a call by Craigie, British Ambassador in Tokyo, on Toyoda on 12th August. Craigie apparently tried to cool the temperature by pleading for an end to "false propaganda." According to Toyoda, Craigie said that: "The British are not doing anything that is threatening to Japan. We cannot increase our forces in Singapore and Malaya because we do not have the ships, although we are increasing aircraft . . . Isn't it to our mutual disadvantage if both our countries engage in false propaganda? In short, Britain is absorbed in defence (50)."

Germany still urged Japan to act against Russia. Tokyo played for time. As Nomura cabled from Washington on the 16th, any more Japanese action could be fatal just now: "Japanese–American relations have today reached a stage in which anything might happen at any moment, and they are likely to grow worse suddenly as soon as Japan makes her next move (51)."

Japanese plans for war against America were still unfinished. *Japan plays* Precious time was needed. On 6th August, Ambassador Nomura *for time* had tried to reopen talks in Washington with new proposals: if normal trade was resumed, Japan would promise not to advance further in south-east Asia. She would pull out of Indochina after the China "Incident," so long as her special status in Indochina was recognized. She would recognize the neutrality of the Philippines.

But Nomura's proposals said nothing about giving up territory already gained. And there were other conditions, too. America must agree to foster direct talks between Japan and China, and to get Japanese access to the natural resources of the south-west Pacific. Finally, America and her "associates" must end any more Far East military preparations.

All this was clearly no good to America. And yet the British and Americans – even more than the Japanese – needed more time. People feared that Japan would now occupy the Kra Isthmus in Thailand, north of the Malayan border, threatening Singapore from the port of Singora.

The British Chiefs of Staff had discussed the issue on 5th *British* August. They wanted to forestall Japan by occupying Singora, *weakness* despite the risk of war and the lack of British strength in the Far East. In June the Cabinet had been told that the forces required to defend the Far East amounted to "two equivalent divisions from the Field Force" plus two divisions of local forces and twenty-two aircraft squadrons. But "the army garrison, though nearly up to strength, is seriously deficient in important items of equipment, notably anti-tank, anti-aircraft and field guns. The present Air Force comprises twelve and one-third squadrons (52).''

On Saturday, 9th August, 1941, a momentous meeting took place off Placentia Bay, Newfoundland. Winston Churchill had sailed from Scapa Flow on board the battleship *Prince of Wales* five days before. Now he began talks with President Roosevelt on board the American cruiser *Augusta*. On the 10th this ''Atlantic Conference'' discussed the rising Japanese menace.

Churchill found that Roosevelt still wanted talks with Japan to go on. But the British Prime Minister had long wanted America and Britain to join in a strong warning to Japan, believing war to be inevitable otherwise. The Cabinet Defence Committee cabled Churchill: ''Situation would be best met by parallel warnings by United States privately to the Japanese Government through the diplomatic channel, to the effect that any incursion by the Japanese forces into Thailand would produce a situation in which we would be compelled to take counter-measures likely to lead to war . . . (53)''

The militant Japanese military leader, Tojo Hideki, was regarded as the inspiration behind Japan's attack on Russia, China and the western Allies

Armed with this telegram, Churchill persuaded Roosevelt to *U.S. note* agree to an American Note being handed to the Japanese Ambassador. Its wording was based closely on the Defence Committee suggestion: "Any further encroachment by Japan in the South-West Pacific would produce a situation in which the United States Government would be compelled to take counter-measures, even though these might lead to war between the United States and Japan (54)."

Churchill sailed home on 14th August, well-satisfied with this *Veiled warning* warning. But disappointment soon came over the note to Japan. Cordell Hull believed the agreed text to be "dangerously strong" and liable to excite Japanese extremists. Roosevelt therefore changed the wording, and the message handed to Ambassador Nomura on 17th August was blunted, with the word "war" carefully avoided: if Japan continued to follow an aggressive policy, America would have "to take any and all steps necessary towards safeguarding the legitimate rights and interests of the United States and American nationals, and towards ensuring the safety and security of the United States (55)."

Churchill was disturbed by this softening of the warning. But the perilous state of Britain's military strength in the Far East was brought home by a grim report to the Chiefs of Staff on 20th August. In August, 1940, it had been decided to entrust the primary Malayan defence to the R.A.F., with a front-line strength of 336 aircraft. Now, a year later, only 180 aircraft were available and most of these were obsolete.

Air Chief Marshall Brooke-Popham, Commander in the Far East, said that the lack of a strong Royal Naval fleet had induced the Chiefs of Staff to rely mainly on aircraft. Yet "we have no reserve air crews and few reserve aircraft . . . This means bluntly that at present not only is our ability to attack shipping deplorably weak, but we have not the staying power to sustain even what we could now do. As our air effort dwindles (as it would, if war came now) so will the enemy's chances of landing increase. Long stretches of beach cannot be defended everywhere, and fighting inland is certain to occur. In these conditions our troops might expect to receive little support from the air (56)."

This warning exposed the full risk in Churchill's attempt to deter the Japanese through threat of war. If the bluff was called, Britain's Far East position would be desperate indeed.

Both America and Japan still tried to avoid treading on one another's toes. Nomura, when he saw Roosevelt on the 17th, suggested a meeting between the President and Prime Minister Konoye. Roosevelt seemed receptive. Konoye therefore sent a cordial message, handed by Nomura to Roosevelt on 28th August. Roosevelt suggested Juneau, Alaska, as a possible meeting place.

Japan's cautious attitude was revealed to the German Ambassador, Ott, in an interview with Foreign Minister Toyoda on 30th August. According to Toyoda, he had told the Ambassador: "There are various ways of preventing American entry into the war. During Matsuoka's time, we tried to deter the Americans with strong language. This aroused the American's hostility, and in the end they severed communications with Japan. Accordingly, we have to think carefully about the pros and cons of getting the United States even more excited (57)."

Japan decides policy

Four days later, the twin Japanese policies of diplomacy and war preparation were combined in a crucial plan, adopted by the Imperial Conference:

"I. Our Empire, for the purposes of self-defence and self-preservation, will complete preparations for war, with the last ten days of October as a tentative deadline, resolved to go to war with the United States, Great Britain and the Netherlands if necessary.

"II. Our Empire will concurrently take all possible diplomatic measures *vis-à-vis* the United States and Great Britain, and thereby endeavour to attain our objectives . . .

"III. If there is no prospect of our demands being met by the first ten days of October . . . we will immediately decide to commence hostilities against the United States, Britain and the Netherlands."

Minimum demands

The minimum diplomatic demands were:

"1. The United States and Great Britain shall neither interfere with nor obstruct the settlement of the China Incident by our Empire. They shall not obstruct our efforts to settle the Incident on the basis of the Fundamental Treaty between Japan and China, and the Joint Declaration of Japan, Manchukuo and China. They shall close the Burma Road and cease to assist the Chiang Kai-shek regime militarily, politically and economically . . .

"2. The United States and Great Britain shall refrain from actions that may threaten the defence of our Empire in the Far East. They shall not secure any military rights in the territories of Thailand, the Netherlands East Indies, China and the Far Eastern section of the Soviet Union. They shall not increase their military forces in the Far East beyond the present strength . . .

"3. The United States and Great Britain shall cooperate in the acquisition of goods needed by our Empire. They shall restore commercial relations with our Empire and supply those goods from their territories in the Southwest Pacific that our Empire urgently needs to sustain herself. They shall amicably contribute to the economic cooperation between Japan, Thailand and the Netherlands East Indies."

After these enormous "minimum" demands came the list of *Japan's* "maximum concessions" which Japan would make if her *"concessions"* demands were met.

"1. Our Empire will not advance militarily from the bases in French Indochina to the neighbouring areas other than China. *Note*: If we are asked about our attitude toward the Soviet Union, we will reply that we will not resort to military force unilaterally unless the Soviet Union violates the Japanese–Soviet Neutrality Pact . . .

"2. Our Empire is prepared to withdraw its forces from French Indochina after a just peace has been established in the Far East.

"3. Our Empire is prepared to guarantee the neutrality of the Philippine Islands (58)."

Few documents can have been more arrogant. Japan wanted *Tokyo's* everything. But she would make no real sacrifices. Her "con- *arrogance* cessions" just amounted to limiting her spoils to those already seized. Other secret parts of her policy documents issued for ministerial guidance showed this arrogance:

"Is the war with Great Britain and the United States inevitable? *War will be* Our Empire's plan to build a New Order in East Asia – the *inevitable* central problem of which is the settlement of the China Incident

63

Japan's aggressive strategy in the Pacific Ocean, 1941–1942

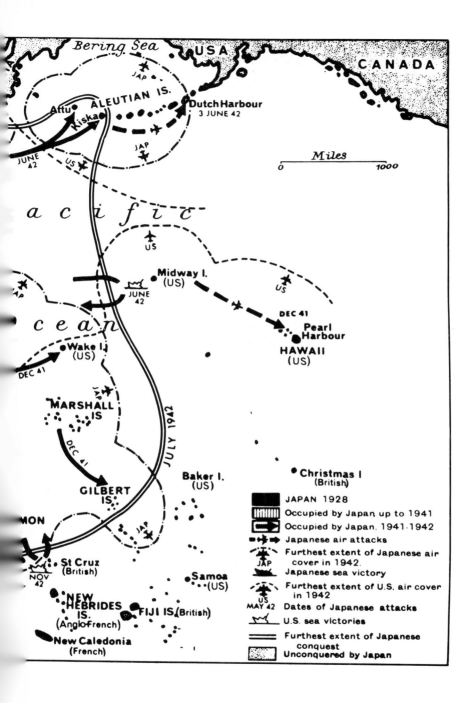

Bering Sea

USA

CANADA

JAP

ALEUTIAN IS.

Attu

Kiska

Dutch Harbour
3 JUNE 42

JUNE
42

US

JAP

Miles

0   1000

Pacific

US

Midway I.
(US)

JUNE
42

US

DEC 41

Ocean

Pearl
Harbour

HAWAII
(US)

Wake I.
(US)

DEC 41

JAP

JULY 1942

MARSHALL
IS.

DEC 41

Baker I.
(US)

Christmas I
(British)

GILBERT
IS.

JAP

JAPAN 1928

Occupied by Japan up to 1941

Occupied by Japan. 1941-1942

Japanese air attacks

Furthest extent of Japanese air
cover in 1942

MON

St Cruz
(British)

NOV
42

Samoa
(US)

JAP

Japanese sea victory

Furthest extent of U.S. air cover
in 1942

Dates of Japanese attacks

U.S. sea victories

NEW
HEBRIDES
IS.
(Anglo-French)

FIJI IS (British)

New Caledonia
(French)

MAY 42

Furthest extent of Japanese
conquest

Unconquered by Japan

– is a firm policy based on the national principle of *Hakko Ichiu*. The building of the New Order will go on forever, much as the life of our State does. However, it appears that the policy of the United States towards Japan is based on the idea of preserving the *status quo*. In order to dominate the world and defend democracy, it aims to prevent our Empire from rising and developing in East Asia . . . The policies of Japan and the United States are mutually incompatible . . . The conflict will ultimately lead to war . . .

War will be long

"*What is the outlook in a war with Great Britain and the United States?* . . . It will become a war of endurance. It is very difficult to predict the termination of war, and it would be well-nigh impossible to expect the surrender of the United States. However . . . the war may end because of a great change in American public opinion, which may result from such factors as the remarkable success of our military operations in the South, or the surrender of Great Britain . . .

Choice of deadline

"*Why have we set the last ten days of October as a tentative deadline for war preparations?* . . . We are now gradually consuming oil that has been stockpiled. If things continue as at present, we will be self-sufficient for a two-year period at the most . . . As time passes, our capacity to carry on war will decline, and our Empire will become powerless militarily. Meanwhile, the naval and air forces of the United States will improve remarkably as time goes on. And defensively, the United States, Great Britain, and the Netherlands will gradually grow stronger in the South . . .

"*When will we resort to military force?* Military force will be used after military preparations have been completed and coordinated, that is, in the early part of November . . . (59)"

Spy in Pearl Harbour

A message from Tokyo intercepted by the U.S. Army on 9th October requested the Japanese agent in Honolulu to send detailed reports on Pearl Harbour. "With regard to warships and aircraft carriers, we would like to have you report on those at anchor – these are not so important – tied up at wharves, buoys and in docks. Designate types and classes briefly. If possible, we would like you to mention when there are two or more vessels along side the same wharf (60)."

Taken by itself, this would seem to give a valuable hint over the coming attack at Pearl Harbour. But at the time, no special significance was attached to the signal: Pearl Harbour was only one of many places about which Japanese agents were asked for information. At the most, the Americans feared minor sabotage attempts.

The proposed meeting between President Roosevelt and Prime Minister Konoye had still to be arranged. Meanwhile, the Japanese Army and Navy had now set 15th October as the deadline. In London, the Foreign Secretary studied the reports reaching the Foreign Office in Whitehall, and wrote on 1st October: "Japan is approaching a serious decision. In my opinion the most likely way to keep her quiet is to convince her that any further adventure on her part will meet with formidable and combined opposition (61)."

Deadline: 15th October

Yet also on 1st October a signal reached London from the Far East which seemed to contradict Anthony Eden's warning: "It must now have become apparent to Japan that war with the United States, Dutch or ourselves, probably means war with all three." Britain and her allies seemed safe for the moment. "Japan is now concentrating her forces against the Russians, and cannot suddenly change this into a concentration in the south (62)."

Eden's Minute to Lord Hankey and this signal – one pessimistic, the other cautiously optimistic – shared a common factor: a belief that Japan could still be deterred. This policy was strongly urged by Churchill and the British Chiefs of Staff. Yet what forces could be used as a deterrent? And what forces were available, should war erupt?

On 2nd October Cordell Hull handed Ambassador Nomura a note reviewing diplomatic developments to date. One paragraph dealt with the argument about Japanese troops in China. A clear sign of "Japan's intention in regard to the withdrawal of Japanese troops from China and French Indochina would be most helpful in making known [her] peaceful intentions . . . in the Pacific area." Hull doubted that a Roosevelt–Konoye meeting would be helpful while the divergence of views continued. And Ambassador Nomura immediately cabled home

Washington Note

that the talks had reached "deadlock."

Military pressure in Tokyo

In Tokyo, Foreign Minister Toyoda wanted to draft a reply to this latest American communication. But the military leaders claimed that no more time could be spared. The Army Chief of Staff, Sugiyama, declared at a Liaison Conference session on 9th October: "The Supreme Command would oppose further delay. If we delay, both the South and the North will be left hanging in the air . . ." Nagano, Navy Chief of Staff, agreed. "There is no longer time for discussion. We want quick action (63)."

Differences between the Japanese Service chiefs and the political leaders still seeking some sort of moderation now reached a critical level. The military deadline for the negotiations would expire on 15th October. On 12th October, the Prime Minister summoned his chief Ministers to his home. There he tried to persuade the War Minister – militant Tojo Hideki – that hope still lay in the talks with America. But Konoye failed to convince Tojo, and another stormy Cabinet meeting took place next morning.

On the same day Nomura in Washington had an urgent cable from the Foreign Minister: "The situation at home is fast approaching a crisis and it is becoming absolutely essential that the two leaders meet if any adjustment of Japanese–U.S. relations is to be accomplished. I cannot go into details now, but please bear this fact in mind (64)."

This cable was intercepted and decoded by the Americans. So too was another signal, sent later during the 13th to Nomura. "Circumstances do not permit even an instant's delay (65)."

Japan's new Prime Minister

But in Tokyo a violent political upheaval had taken place. War Minister Tojo had forced the more moderate Prince Konoye to resign. Tojo himself was summoned by the Emperor and told: "We direct you to form a Cabinet and to abide by the provisions of the Constitution. We believe that an exceedingly grave situation confronts the nation. Bear in mind, at this time, that cooperation between the Army and Navy should be closer than ever before (66)."

And so the tough General Tojo became Prime Minister, while still keeping his powerful position as Minister of War. He was almost a dictator. Moderates in the Japanese Cabinet were subdued or forced out. Military pressure to plunge into war with America and Britain now had political backing.

A wave of renewed alarm swept through the western capitals when news arrived of Tojo's appointment.

5 Hakko Ichiu

"THE FALL of Prince Konoye's Government is an ominous sign," wrote Anthony Eden to Winston Churchill. "We discussed some little time ago the possibility of capital ship reinforcements to the Far East. The matter has now become more urgent, and I should be glad if it could be discussed at the Defence Committee tomorrow afternoon (67)."

Churchill had already urged that modern battleships should be sent, such as the *Prince of Wales*. But the Admiralty had thought it too risky, and preferred the older R-class vessels. Yet Churchill declared at the Defence Committee meeting on 17th October:

"The presence of one modern capital ship in Far Eastern waters could be calculated to have a [deterrent] effect on the Japanese naval authorities, and thereby on Japanese foreign policy." He reminded the Committee that the modern battleship *Repulse* had already reached the Indian Ocean. "No time should now be lost in sending the *Prince of Wales* to join up with her at Singapore."

Eden agreed, and added: "If the *Prince of Wales* were to call at Cape Town on her way to the Far East, news of her movements would quickly reach Japan and the deterrent effect would begin." Under this pressure from the Prime Minister and Foreign Secretary the Committee agreed with the sailing of the *Prince of Wales*, initially to Cape Town. She left on Saturday, 25th October, flying the flag of Admiral Sir Tom Phillips (68).

Four days later a worrying report reached London from Duff Cooper, who had been sent out to the Far East in August. He

71

Japanese armoured vehicles cross the causeway into Singapore – a brilliant diversionary move to distract American and British attention from fleet movements towards the Hawaiian islands now revealed Britain's Far East possessions were even less prepared for war in civil matters than they were in the military sphere.

Tokyo: another delay Meanwhile, in Tokyo the new Prime Minister, Tojo, unexpectedly restrained the extremists in his Cabinet. Emperor Hirohito probably wanted the issue of war versus talks set down in black and white to present a clear case to the moderates that war was inevitable. But Nagano, the Navy Chief of Staff, objected to the new delay, complaining to the Liaison Conference on 23rd October:

"We were to have reached a decision in October, and yet here we are. So I want to see our study and discussion kept concise. The Navy is consuming 400 tons of oil an hour. The situation is urgent." Sugiyama, the Army Chief, agreed: "Things have already been delayed one month. We can't devote four or five days to study. Hurry up and go ahead (69)."

For the next week a succession of meetings re-examined the whole war question. But by the end of the month these sessions were nearing completion – and the military leaders increased their pressure for an early decision. Even at this time Churchill was cabling Roosevelt:

"I think myself that Japan is more likely to drift into war than to plunge in (70)."

Japan fixes war date Ironically, only next day – 1st November – the Japanese Liaison Conference met for a historic 17-hour session which decided upon a definite date for war. Tension ran high, with discussion degenerating into angry, shouted exchanges. The Japanese leaders were called upon to choose one of three alternatives: peace, war, or war qualified by continuing negotiations until an absolute deadline of 30th November. The War, Navy and other Ministers favoured the last alternative, except for the Foreign Minister who was uncertain. But the Army Staff strongly urged for the second choice – war now, without further diplomatic discussions.

The Navy agreed to extend the deadline for negotiations until 20th November, and the Army Vice-Chief of Staff, Tsukada, reluctantly stated that talks could perhaps continue until 13th November, but definitely no later. Foreign Minister Togo was angry at this effort to force the pace of diplomatic talks: "You say there must be a deadline for diplomacy. As Foreign Minister, I cannot engage in diplomacy unless there is a prospect that it will be successful. I cannot accept deadlines or conditions if they make it unlikely that diplomacy will succeed. . . . November 13th is outrageous. The Navy says November 20th."

And so the rowdy, fateful, discussion continued. Eventually, after a 20-minute recess to allow tempers to cool, the Army Chief of Staff agreed that "it would be all right to carry on negotiations until 30th November." Prime Minister Tojo then asked:

"Can't we make it 1st December? Can't you allow diplomatic negotiations to go on even for one day more?

Tsukada: "Absolutely not. We absolutely can't go beyond November 30th. Absolutely not."

Shimada: "Mr. Tsukada, until what time on the 30th? It will be all right until midnight, won't it?"

Tsukada: "It will be all right until midnight (71)."

In this noisy fashion the deadline was set at midnight, 30th November, Tokyo time. Negotiations would continue until that moment.

Also, on 1st November, Admiral Yamamoto – Commander of the Japanese Combined Fleet – completed his "Top Secret Operation Order No. 1." He intended "to drive Britain and America from Greater East Asia, and to hasten the settlement of the China Incident . . . When Britain and America have been driven from the Netherlands Indies and the Philippines, [a new] economic entity will be firmly established. The vast and far-reaching fundamental principle, the goal of our nation – *Hakko Ichiu* – will be demonstrated to the world."

War orders

Yamamoto gave details of the overall war plan. First, Thailand would be invaded and air strikes would be delivered at the Malay Peninsula and on Luzon in the Philippines. And a carrier-borne force would launch a massive air attack on the U.S. Pacific Fleet at Pearl Harbour. Then would come the conquest of the Philippines, Borneo, British Malaya including Singapore, and Sumatra. Japanese amphibious forces would follow these victories by converging upon Java in the Dutch

73

Overleaf Denied vital aircraft protection, H.M.S. *Prince of Wales* became a victim of Japan's deadly and effective air force

Indies. A "ribbon defence" would be established by securing territory stretching from the Kurile Islands through Wake, the Marshalls and around the southern and western edges of the Malay Barrier to the Burmese–Indian border. A naval striking force would disrupt sea communications westward and southward from Hawaii, Panama, and the West Coast of South America.

Choice of routes
This Operation Order No. 1 resulted from hours of staff study during the previous two months. The details of an attack on Pearl Harbour had been closely worked out. First of all, planners had had to decide on the route for the aircraft carrier Strike Force. Three routes had been examined. The Strike Force could sail south through the Marshalls; this, like the central course heading east from Japan then southward of the line Midway–Oahu, would lead through relatively calm waters, making re-fuelling at sea easier. The northern route, between the Aleutians and Midway, would pass through harsh seas, making re-fuelling harder.

But the southern and central courses were more open to view from merchantmen and American patrol aircraft. The northern route was finally chosen, despite the sea hazards. On 5th October about 100 pilot officers from the carrier air groups had been summoned to a meeting on board the *Akagi* anchored off Shibushi. These favoured few had been told of their selection for the Pearl Harbour attack (72). So Admiral Yamamoto put the final touches to his plan and submitted the document to Admiral Nagano, Chief of the Naval Staff, on 1st November.

A signal decoded
Almost at once the Americans had new evidence that diplomacy was nearly over. An intercepted cable from Tokyo to the Washington Embassy, dated 2nd November, declared: "We have carefully considered a fundamental policy for improving relations between Japan and America, but we expect to reach a final decision in a meeting on the morning of the 5th and will let you know the result at once." This meeting scheduled for 5th November was the rowdy Imperial Conference session, needed to give final approval to the Liaison Conference decision taken on 1st November. The cable to Washington continued: "This will be our Government's last effort to improve diplomatic

relations. The situation is very grave . . . (73)"

This signal was studied in a top-level discussion on 3rd November in Washington, attended by America's military chiefs. Unfortunately, they came to a tragically wrong conclusion. According to the official minutes: "General Marshall felt that the main involvement in the Far East would be naval and that . . . the Navy was now fighting a battle in the Atlantic." He felt "that the Japanese authorities had not as yet determined the action to be taken under the present situation." He was informed "that the Japanese authorities might be expected to decide upon the national policy by November 5th . . . It was his belief that as long as the augmented Army Air Force remained in the Philippines, Japanese action against the south would be a very hazardous operation. It was his belief that by the middle of December, the Army forces in the Philippines would be of impressive strength, and this in itself would have a deterrent effect on Japanese operations (74)." *Marshall's mistake*

And yet on this same Sunday the Japanese Chief of Naval Staff gave his approval to the Operations Plan submitted by Admiral Yamamoto two days before, specifying attacks on targets throughout the Far East. Nagano hurried to the Emperor's palace with Sugiyama, his army colleague. *Target dates*

"What is the Navy's target date?" asked the Emperor Hirohito.

Nagano replied: "December 8th."

"Isn't that a Monday?" asked Hirohito.

"We chose it," said Nagano, "because everyone will be tired after the weekend (75)."

And also on 3rd November the American Ambassador in Tokyo warned Cordell Hull, U.S. Secretary of State, against "any possible misconception of the capacity of Japan to rush headlong into a suicidal conflict with the United States. National sanity would dictate against such an event, but Japanese sanity cannot be measured by our own standards of logic (76)." American and British leaders would have done well to heed this perceptive advice from Ambassador Grew.

Next day, 4th November, the Japanese Ambassador in Washington was again told by Tokyo: "We have decided . . . to

77

The battleship *Huso* leads a Japanese battle squadron off the coast of Malaya

gamble once more on the continuance of the parleys. But this is our last effort. Both in name and spirit this counter-proposal of our's is, indeed, the last. I want you to know that. If through it we do not reach a quick accord, I am sorry to say the talks will certainly be ruptured. Then, indeed, will relations between our two nations be on the brink of chaos (77)."

Tokyo's plans   As American experts decoded this signal, a long meeting of the Imperial Conference took place in Tokyo. The meeting was to put the final stamp of approval on the decision for war. During the discussion, Hara, President of the Privy Council, declared: "I should like both the Army and Navy Chiefs of Staff to explain what will happen if the negotiations break down. Please state it in such a way that it can be understood with the use of common sense. Regarding operations in the South, the field of battle in the map we have here covers the entire region. What is the scope of operations, and how successful are our military operations likely to be?"

Sugiyama: "Targets of this operation are military and air bases in Guam, Hong Kong, British Malaya, Burma, British Borneo, Dutch Borneo, Sumatra, Celebes, the Bismarck Islands, and small islands south-west of the Bismarck Islands. The numerical strength of the enemy in these places is more than 200,000, while the number of enemy aircraft is 800. There are other forces in India, Australia, and New Zealand, which I assume would participate sooner or later.

"The Army will carry out operations under these conditions in co-operation with the Navy, and its major efforts will be made in the Philippines and Malaya. The operation is planned to start in Malaya and the Philippines simultaneously, and then to move towards the Netherland East Indies. In this way, it is estimated that it will take 50 days to complete the operations in the Philippines, 100 days in Malaya, and 50 days in the Netherlands East Indies . . . The entire operation will be completed within five months after the opening of the war . . . (78)"

Members of the Imperial Conference sat in shocked astonishment as Sugiyama's pointer ranged over the map to reveal to the awesome extent of the Japanese war plan. Pearl Harbour barely received a mention: this American base merely featured as one target in a seemingly endless list. *A huge attack*

Prime Minister Tojo ended the conference with these words: "As to what our moral basis for going to war should be, there is some merit in making it clear that Great Britain and the United States represent a strong threat to Japan's self-preservation. Also, if we are fair in governing the occupied areas, attitudes towards us would probably relax. America may be enraged for a while, but later she will come to understand. In any case I will be careful to avoid the war becoming a racial war.

"Do you have any other comments? If not I will rule that the proposals have been approved in their original form (79)." No comments came from the conference. All those present looked at the solemn-faced Emperor for guidance. Hirohito gave a slight nod. Japan had at last taken her formal decision to go to war.

In London, Churchill's Ministers met next day, 5th Nov- *British fears* ember, to hear a disturbing report from Sir Earle Page, special Australian envoy to the British Government. Page warned that Australia was worried about the lack of air strength at Singapore. Nine months ago, he said, it had been estimated that the minimum air strength required at Singapore was 336 aircraft. "We now have 130 in the front line."

Churchill replied that the airforce had indeed grown more slowly than hoped. Aircraft had to be sent to help the struggling Russians, to the Middle East, and some kept at home in case of a German invasion attempt. But the Prime Minister claimed that the lack in air strength was partly made up by naval reinforcements bound for the Far East. "We had taken some risk in detaching the *Prince of Wales* from the Home Fleet. The *Prince of Wales* was now on her way to Cape Town and likely to proceed to Singapore (80)."

Weak Pacific fleet   American leaders also had worrying reports of military strength in the Far East. On this same day the U.S. Joint Board pointed out that their Pacific Fleet remained inferior to the Japanese Fleet and could not fight a major offensive unless all warships were withdrawn from the Atlantic. American naval and air strength was gradually increasing in the Philippines, and by mid-December would become a positive threat to any Japanese move south of Formosa; but not until March, 1942, would it be a decisive weapon (81).

Japanese ultimatum   War could now only be averted by an American acceptance of the latest Japanese diplomatic demands (see page 62). These were transmitted to Ambassador Nomura in Washington on 5th November, together with this message intercepted by the Americans: "It is absolutely necessary that all arrangements for the signing of this agreement be completed by the 25th of this month. I realize that this is a difficult order, but under the circumstances it is an unavoidable one (82)."

Another telegram to Nomura later that day added: "Time is becoming exceedingly short and the situation very critical. Absolutely no delays can be permitted. Please bear this in mind and do your best. I wish to stress this point over and over (83)."

Nomura meets Hull   Ambassador Nomura had been instructed to offer Proposal A, then, if this failed, to present B. He accordingly saw Cordell Hull

80

Opposite H.M.S. *Repulse's* blazing guns proved useless on 11th December, 1941, when she was sunk by Japanese bombers on 7th November with Proposal A, and pressed for a quick American response. This reply had still to arrive by 10th November. This was the day on which Admiral Yamamoto told Admiral Nagumo Chu-ichi – commanding the Pearl Harbour attack fleet – to make his ships' captains "complete battle preparations by November 20th".

Also on 10th November the Chief of Staff of the Combined Fleet, Rear Admiral Ito, gave the Strike Force flag officers a rousing address: "A gigantic fleet . . . has massed in Pearl Harbour. This fleet will be utterly crushed with one blow at the very beginning of hostilities . . . If these plans should fail at any stage, our Navy will suffer the wretched fate of never being able to rise again. The success of our surprise attack on Pearl Harbour will prove to be the Waterloo of the war to follow. For this reason the Imperial Navy is massing the cream of its strength in ships and planes to assure success . . . If we insure our strategic supremacy at the very outset . . . by attacking and seizing all key points at one blow while America is still unprepared, we

can swing the scales of later operations in our favour. Heaven will bear witness to the righteousness of our struggle (84)."

Winston Churchill rose to speak at the annual Guildhall banquet in the City of London. He peered over his spectacles at the dignitaries before him. He growled that if American forces became involved in war with Japan, "It is my duty to say that the British declaration will follow within the hour." Next day, 11th November, five days before reaching Cape Town, the *Prince of Wales* was ordered to proceed to Ceylon and then to Singapore with the *Repulse*. The decision to send these two great battleships – the pride of the Royal Navy – to the Far East was now even more hazardous: the British aircraft carrier *Indomitable*, which was to have accompanied the warships to provide essential air protection, had run aground off Jamaica on the 3rd, and could not be with them.

Nomura still awaited the American reply to Proposal A. Another message to the Ambassador – intercepted by the Americans on the 11th – re-emphasized the need for speed: "Judging from the progress of the conversations, it seems that the United States is still not fully aware of the exceedingly criticalness [*sic*] of the situation here (85)."

In Tokyo the Japanese Foreign Minister summoned the U.S. Ambassador, Grew, and complained about the absence of an American reply. He told Grew: "The United States has delayed and delayed. Japan has made concession after concession . . . Since the United States is applying economic pressure on us, which is even stronger than military pressure, we may have to act in order to defend ourselves. For the United States to insist that Japan disregard the sacrifices she is making in China is tantamount to telling us to commit suicide. Please convey this to your Government."

Grew replied: "I understand. I will convey it to my Government. I am most anxious to find a solution (86)." Grew went home in a tearful mood, according to Toyoda's accounts.

Next morning, 16th November, a special Japanese envoy arrived in Washington to try and hurry things. The envoy, Kurusu Saburo, was to tell Roosevelt and Hull that Japan no longer bluffed. If the Americans dragged out negotiations beyond the deadline of 25th he must secretly inform the Japanese Embassy in Washington of the decision which had been reached in Tokyo to go to war.

When at last Hull rejected Proposal A, Kurusu and Nomura went away to prepare the second, and only, alternative. Proposal B demanded a return to the position before Japan's takeover of south Indochina, and America's subsequent freezing of Japanese assets. Nomura still pleaded with Tokyo for more time, but the Foreign Minister replied: "I am awfully sorry to say that the situation renders this out of the question. I set the deadline for the solution of these negotiations, and there will be no change. Please try to understand that (87)." Kurusu paid his first formal visit on Roosevelt on 17th November and had more talks with Hull on the 18th: he hinted at Proposal B without officially presenting it for the moment.

On the same day the last warships of the Strike Force sailed from Kure naval base on the Inland Sea of Japan. All ships kept strict radio silence from the time of departure. The rest of the Combined Fleet at Kure increased their radio communication, so that American monitors would not be alarmed by any reduction in radio traffic. *Japanese fleet sails*

This trick worked. But the American signal stations did intercept two revealing messages next day, 19th November. These emphasized the critical international situation. Tokyo evidently wished to prepare agents and diplomats for a sudden rupture in relations with America, Britain and Russia. A special code had therefore been evolved, as described in this signal – the second signal repeated the instructions more briefly:

"Regarding the broadcast of a special message in an emergency. In case of emergency (danger of cutting of our diplomatic relations), and the cutting off of international communications, the following warning will be added in the middle of the daily Japanese language short-wave news broadcast.

"1. In case of Japan–U.S. relations in danger: *Higashi no kaseame* (east wind rain). 2. Japan–U.S.S.R. relations: *Kitanokaze kumori* (north wind cloudy). 3. Japan–British relations: *Nishi no kaze hare* (west wind clear) . . . When this is heard please destroy all codes, etc. (88)."

Proposal B These famous "wind-code" messages led to special orders being sent to U.S. monitoring stations. Personnel were told to listen out for the code names and report them urgently if they were transmitted. This transmission might come at any moment. Nomura formally presented Proposal B to Hull on 20th November, and the American reaction was extremely cool. Included in Proposal B was a demand that the United States agree to provide Japan with oil. Another section insisted that America "undertakes to refrain from such measures and action as will be prejudicial to the endeavours for the restoration of general peace between Japan and China." In other words, America must stop sending aid to Chiang Kai-shek (89).

Hull later described his reaction to the Japanese demands. They were "of so preposterous a character that no responsible American official could ever have dreamed of accepting." America was being asked to agree to "virtually a surrender (90)." Yet Roosevelt and his advisers knew from the "Magic" interceptions that Proposal B must be regarded as the last Japanese bid to avert war through diplomatic means. Outright rejection must mean conflict.

Hull's reply Cordell Hull set about drafting an American reply, which he managed to complete in 24 hours. The result showed a remarkable willingness to meet the Japanese at least half way. Japan would be asked to agree to a withdrawal of armed forces in southern Indochina and to end military activities there, and "to limit Japanese military forces in northern French Indochina to the number there on 26th July, 1941, which number in any case would not exceed 25,000 and which number would not be subject to replacement." In return, America would undertake "to remove the freezing restrictions which were placed on Japanese assets in the United States on 26th July." America would ask Britain and Holland to take similar steps

Hull's reply went on: "The Government of the United States would not look with disfavour upon the inauguration of conversations between the Government of China and the Government of Japan directed toward a peaceful settlement of their difference. Nor . . . upon an armistice during the period of any such discussions." This *modus vivendi* would last for three months unless renewed by common agreement (91).

Hull showed this draft document to the British and Chinese Ambassadors on 22nd November. The latter, according to Hull's report, "was somewhat disturbed, as he always is when any question concerning China arises not entirely to his way of thinking (92)." This concern soon multiplied.

Meanwhile, on the same day, the Americans intercepted another message from Tokyo. Nomura had apparently repeated his plea for more time, and now the Foreign Minister wired reluctant agreement: "There are reasons beyond your ability to guess why we wanted to settle Japanese–American relations by the 25th, but if within the next three or four days you can finish your conversations with the Americans, if the signing can be completed by the 29th (let me write it out for you – twenty-ninth) . . . we have decided to wait until that date. This time we mean it, that the deadline cannot be changed. After that things are automatically going to happen (93)." *Japan delays again*

Despite knowledge of this extension of the deadline, American forces were told by Washington to be prepared for imminent action. A warning despatch sent from the Chief of Naval Operations to the Commander-in-Chief, Pacific Fleet, on 24th November declared: *America prepares for war*

"Chances of favourable outcome of negotiations with Japan very doubtful. This situation coupled with statements of Japanese Government and movements of their naval and military forces indicate in our opinion that a surprise aggressive movement in any direction including attack on Philippines or Guam is a possibility. Chief of Staff has seen this despatch concurs . . . Utmost secrecy necessary in order not to complicate an already tense situation or precipitate Japanese action (94)."

All seemed to depend upon the American reaction to the Proposal B, and, in the relatively mild form drafted by Hull, chances of acceptance by Tokyo might just be possible. Also on 24th November Roosevelt sent Churchill an outline of this draft counter-proposal. Roosevelt commented in his signal: "This seems to me a fair proposition for the Japanese, but its acceptance or rejection is really a matter of internal Japanese politics. I am not very hopeful and we must all be prepared for real trouble, possibly soon (95)."

Churchill's
comment

Churchill criticized the draft, in a reply to Roosevelt which reached Washington late next day. "Of course it is for you to handle this business, and we certainly do not want an additional war. There is only one point that disquiets me. What about Chiang Kai-shek? Is he not having a very thin diet (96)?"

American
War Council

A drastic change of attitude had started to take place in Washington. According to Stimson's diary Roosevelt had warned his War Council "we were likely to be attacked perhaps next Monday, for the Japanese are notorious for making an attack without warning. The question was how we should manoeuvre them into a position of firing the first shot without allowing too much danger to ourselves. It was a difficult proposition. Hull laid out his general broad propositions on which the thing should be rested – the freedom of the seas and the fact that Japan was in alliance with Hitler and was carrying out his policy of world aggression. The others brought out the fact that any such expedition to the South as the Japanese were likely to take would be an encirclement of our interests in the Philippines and cutting into our vital supplies of rubber from Malaya."

Stimson "pointed out to the President that he had already taken the first steps towards an ultimatum in notifying Japan way back last summer that if she crossed the border into Thailand she was violating our safety and that therefore he had only to point out [to Japan] that to follow any such expedition was a violation of a warning we had already given. So Hull is to go to work on preparing that (97)."

Stimson's diary entry, especially the last sentence, shows the important change in American policy which was soon to come to the forefront. Chiang Kai-shek too had made known his violent objections. He declared: "Chinese national trust in America would be undermined by reports of Japan's escaping military defeat by diplomatic victory (98)."

News of
enemy troops

And now, in this uneasy, critical situation, Hull received intelligence reports of Japanese troop movements. Henry Stimson had been handed these reports soon after returning to his office from the War Council session; the U.S. War Secretary noted in his diary: "Five divisions have come down from Shantung and Shansi to Shanghai and there they had embarked on ships – 30, 40 or 50 ships – and have been sighted south of Formosa (99)."

Alarm shook London and Washington; when Roosevelt learned of the movement from Stimson early on 26th November "he fairly blew up – jumped up into the air, so to speak, and said . . . that that changed the whole situation because it was an evidence of bad faith on the part of the Japanese that while they were negotiating for an entire truce – an entire withdrawal . . . they should be sending this expedition down there to Indochina (100)."

Unknown to the Americans the destination of the force was British Malaya, not Indochina. And the movement had been made deliberately conspicuous to attract attention from the departure of other attack fleets: at 0900 on 26th November, after final preparations had been made, the Strike Force for Pearl Harbour slipped away in thick fog from the isolated Tankan Bay on Etorofu, biggest of the Kurile Islands. Six aircraft carriers sailed in two parallel columns escorted by cruisers and destroyers and battleships. Other destroyers steamed in front to detect and clear away shipping in order to preserve secrecy. Any American, British or Dutch vessels would be sunk on sight, while neutral ships would be boarded and radio transmissions blocked. A careful and continuous check was made on radio signals from Pearl Harbour, to find out if the secret had been discovered, but signals traffic seemed normal.

Japanese fleet sails for Pearl Harbour

Thus the silent departure had gone unnoticed. But in Washington the news of the sighting of the other force had more repercussions. Hull met Roosevelt early on the 26th, and the Americans now decided to scrap Hull's moderate draft proposals. Instead the Japanese would be handed an infinitely tougher statement. This new Ten Point Note, had the following uncompromising requirements: "The Government of Japan will withdraw all military, naval, air and police force from China and from Indochina.

Ten Point Note

"The Government of the United States and the Government

87

of Japan will not support [any] government or regime in China other than the National Government of the Republic of China . . .

"Both Governments will agree that no agreement which either has concluded with any third power or powers shall be intercepted by it in such a way as to conflict with the fundamental purpose of this agreement, the establishment and preservation of peace throughout the Pacific area (101)."

In other words, instead of allowing up to 25,000 Japanese troops in Indochina, or even the mere 5,000 sought by the Chinese, all would have to go. Chiang Kai-shek's Government would have to be recognized by Tokyo. And the American statement attacked the Japanese–German Pact. In return America would agree to discussions on a trade agreement with Japan, Japanese assets in America would be unfrozen, and the money rate between the two countries would be stabilized.

The Ten Point Note therefore set forth America's maximum demands. The document clearly stemmed from the criticisms of the first draft proposed by Hull, from the War Council meeting on 25th November, and from the latest reports of Japanese troops movements – which showed the Americans that the Japanese were already acting in bad faith. But the Ten Point Note could not possibly be accepted by the Japanese. The last chances of peace – already extremely frail – had been shattered.

Point of no return Hull went to see the Japanese Ambassador later in the day to hand over the Note, but even before this Nomura had discovered the general contents of the document and reported back to Tokyo. Emperor Hirohito declared to his Lord Privy Seal: "Although it is with deep regret and anxiety, I am forced to admit that we have reached the point of no return."

6 Fall of Peace

CORDELL HULL, U.S. Secretary of State, was nearing the point of total exhaustion. He was desperately tired after the weeks and months of seemingly endless negotiations. Round and round had gone the talks in the stale Washington atmosphere. His eyes were red-rimmed, his nerves were stretched to snapping point, his patience and endurance had almost reached their limits. But now the endless circle had been severed: during the evening of 26th November, Hull presented Nomura and Kurusu with his drastic Ten Point Note. The two Japanese envoys immediately signalled Tokyo: "We were both dumbfounded . . . We argued back furiously but Hull remained solid as a rock." They had requested, and obtained, an interview with Roosevelt for the following afternoon. *Hull exhausted*

The weary Hull spoke to Stimson, U.S. War Secretary, on Thursday morning, 27th November, and admitted: "I have washed my hands of it and it is now in the hands of you and Knox – the Army and the Navy."

On the same day Admiral Stark, Chief of Naval Operations, urged more time to build up requisite strength: "If the current negotiations end without agreement, Japan may attack the Burma Road, Thailand, Malaya, the Netherlands East Indies, the Philippines, the Russian Maritime Provinces. Precipitance of military action on our part should be avoided so long as consistent with national policy. The longer the delay, the more positive becomes the assurance of retention of [the Philippines] as a naval and air base (102)." *U.S. Navy wants more time*

Yet time had almost run out. And also on this Thursday –

As Japanese shells splash into the sea nearby, aircraft scramble to action aboard the U.S. carrier *Kitkum Bay*, in an engagement off the Philippines

Thanksgiving Day in America – Stark signalled the Commander-in-Chief, Pacific Fleet: "This despatch is to be considered a war warning. Negotiations with Japan looking toward stabilization of conditions in the Pacific have ceased, and an aggressive move by Japan is expected within the next few days. The number and equipment of Japanese troops, and the organization of naval task forces, indicates an amphibious expedition against either the Philippines, Thai or Kra Peninsula, or possibly Borneo. Execute an appropriate defensive deployment . . . Inform district and Army authorities. A similar warning is being sent by War Department (103)."

Pearl Harbour quiet

There was a crucial absence of direct reference to Pearl Harbour. A Japanese move towards Pearl Harbour would, it was believed, be easily detected, and once discovered would be extremely vulnerable to U.S. counter-attack. Pearl Harbour seemed fairly secure – although one big precaution was taken: the three aircraft carriers at the base were ordered to

90

leave, together with half the Army aircraft. The prime target had therefore been removed, but a massive fleet of battleships remained.

Nomura and Kurusu met Roosevelt on the 27th. The President proved as stubborn as his Secretary of State had been the day before. The anxious Japanese Foreign Office telephoned Kurusu late in the evening to find out the result; the Japanese envoy spoke to an official in Tokyo named Yamamoto. American evesdroppers heard this conversation. The code would have been comical if the content had not been so critical.

Yamamoto: "How did the matrimonial question [negotiations] get along today?"

Kurusu: "Oh, haven't you got our telegram yet?... There wasn't much that was different from what Miss Umeko [Cordell Hull] intimated yesterday."

Yamamoto: "Really? Not much different?"

Kurusu: "No, not much. As before that southward matter, that south, south, southward matter [the detected movement of Japanese naval transports, believed to be heading for Indochina] is having considerable effect. You know? Southward matter?"

Yamamoto: "Ah so! The south matter? It's having an effect?"

Kurusu: "Yes, and at one time the matrimonial question seemed as if it would be settled. But well, of course, there are other matters involved too. However, that was it: That was the monkey wrench... How do things look there? Does it seem as if a child might be born? [A decision taken.]"

Yamamoto: "Yes, the birth of the child seems imminent."

Kurusu: "Oh it does? It does seem as if the birth is going to take place? [Pause] In what direction? [Pause] I mean – is it to be a boy or a girl? [War or Peace]."

Yamamoto: "It seems as if it will be a strong healthy boy."

Kurusu: "Oh! It's to be a strong healthy boy?"

Yamamoto: "Yes..."

Kurusu: "Well. I suppose there's nothing more that can be done then."

Yamamoto: "Well yes... The matrimonial question, that is, the matter pertaining to arranging a marriage – don't break them off.''

Kurusu: "Not break them? You mean talks? [Pause] Oh my! [Pause] Er. Well. I'll do what I can . . . (104)"

This confusion shown by the special Japanese envoy seems understandable. Continued discussions were only meant as a cover for the final military preparations – and to let the Pearl Harbour Strike Force reach its position.

Signals for action

The Americans were now fully aware that further talks would only be sham. Information flashed to area commanders, with Admiral Stark signalling the Pacific Fleet on 28th November: "Army has sent following to commander western defence command. Negotiations with Japan appear to be terminated to all practical purposes with only the barest possibilities that the Japanese Government might come back and offer to continue. Japanese future action unpredictable, but hostile action possible at any moment. If hostilities cannot – repeat cannot – be avoided the United States desires that Japan commit the first overt act . . . Prior to hostile Japanese action you are directed to undertake such reconnaissance and other measures as you deem necessary but these measures should be carried out so as not repeat not to alarm civil population or disclose intent (105)."

Pearl Harbour seems secure

At Pearl Harbour itself precautions were still limited to checks on sabotage attempts. No stronger form of Japanese attack seemed likely. Both Army and Navy continued to operate under the limited alert conditions that had been observed throughout 1941. And in Washington, at a meeting between Roosevelt and his War Cabinet on the 28th, Pearl Harbour failed to find a mention. Instead, the Americans considered a personal appeal from Roosevelt to Hirohito. An attack on the distant base on Oahu Island seemed an extremely remote threat. Surely it would be too suicidal, even for the Japanese. And there was no sign of naval movements towards the Hawaiian Islands, despite many reconnaissance patrols.

Japanese Strike Force

The Japanese Strike Force battled through terrible seas. Giant waves washed men overboard and battered the massive warships. Wind shrieked across the carrier flight decks and wailed through the rigging. Black clouds boiled above. And this harsh weather, as intended, helped the Japanese escape detec-

The weapons on which the battle of the Pacific depended: aircraft, guns
and shells

tion. Supremely confident, the Japanese sailed on.

British Ministers were told that the reported Japanese move
southwards, possibly against Thailand, had led to an exchange
of telegrams with the Dominions Governments. The Japanese
convoy had put in at Hainan, where it had remained for the
moment. But the British Commander-in-Chief, Far East, had
still sought permission to move into the Kra Isthmus if Japanese
warships were found nearing this strategic section of Thailand.
He was supported by the Australians. The British Chiefs of
Staff, on the other hand, feared the operation would spark off
war, and should be avoided so long as uncertainty remained
over full American support.

Churchill then told the War Cabinet that "we ought not to
assume that the outbreak of war between England and Japan
*Churchill's
caution* 93

would necessarily precipitate the United States into the war. There was a strong party in the United States who would work up prejudice against being drawn into Britain's war . . . We should not resist or attempt to forestall a Japanese attack on the Kra Isthmus, unless we had a satisfactory assurance from the United States that they would join us should our attack cause us to become involved in war with Japan." Ministers agreed (106).

And so Britain, like America – although for different reasons – delayed taking full defensive precautions. Ironically, the Americans had just decoded a Japanese plan to entice the British to invade Thailand and so permit Japan to enter that country as a "defender". On the same day, Japanese radio call signs suddenly changed – these signs were used to identify senders and receivers of radio messages. According to the American intelligence report, it "indicates an additional progressive step in preparing for active operations on a large scale (107)."

Next day the intelligence unit added: "Almost a complete blank of information on the [Japanese] carriers today." These colossal warships had disappeared. Yet on 2nd December Admiral Yamamoto broadcast a prearranged code from his flagship in the Inland Sea to the Strike Force proceeding towards Pearl Harbour: *"Niitaka Yama Nobore"* – "Climb Mount Niitaka". This meant "Proceed with Attack." 8th December was confirmed as X-Day. The Japanese steamed on far into the Pacific.

On the same day the ill-fated *Prince of Wales* and *Repulse* reached Singapore. War Cabinet and Defence Committee discussions had mainly been about the value of these warships as a deterrent. Deterrence was now too late. Should hostilities start the battleships would be very vulnerable without proper air protection. Although unaware of just how close Britain and Japan stood to war, Admiralty fears had increased. A last minute attempt was now made to rescue the warships from danger: a signal was made late on the 2nd to Admiral Phillips, commander of the fleet, suggesting he should order the *Prince of Wales* and *Repulse* to leave Singapore. Preparations were made for the vessels to sail on the 5th.

During Wednesday, 3rd December, the Japanese Strike Force reached a point about 2,300 miles northwest of Pearl Harbour. Seas had moderated and, in a light swell, the carriers took on oil from the accompanying tankers. These slower supply vessels, and an escort of short-range destroyers, then turned back towards Japan, leaving the fast carriers and long-range escort to proceed with their dash to Hawaii. Progress could now be swift. *Japanese fleet speeds up*

The Americans remained without the slightest evidence as to where the carriers were. Yet hints at an early outbreak of war increased. The Commander-in-Chief, Pacific Fleet, received this signal on 3rd December:

"Highly reliable information has been received that categoric and urgent instructions were sent yesterday to Japanese diplomatic and consular posts at Hong Kong, Singapore, Batavia, Manila, Washington and London to destroy most of their codes and ciphers at once and to burn all other important confidential and secret documents (108)."

At last, on the following day, Britain's War Cabinet learned what was in the Ten Point Note handed by Hull to Nomura more than a week before. Ministers immediately agreed the stern points were "very satisfactory." But this tough line had been sought by Britain as part of the outdated deterrent policy.

The War Cabinet also heard that Roosevelt had approved a statement that "in the event of any direct attack on ourselves or the Dutch, we should obviously all be in it together." This seemed to imply a promise of American support in a war against the Japanese. Churchill thought that the Commander-in-Chief, Far East, could now be ordered to move into Thailand's Kra Isthmus if necessary. The words "if necessary" were to bring unfortunate complications. The Commander, Sir Robert Brooke-Popham, felt uncertain as to how far he was actually free to act. The operation was thus delayed for three fatal days from 5th to 8th December (109). *"In it together"*

On Friday morning, 5th December, the Japanese transports sailed from their waiting point at Samah harbour, Hainan, and began the final run for Thailand and Malaya. In contrast to the

Despite the frequent allied air-patrols, the Japanese strike force sailed undetected towards Pearl Harbour.

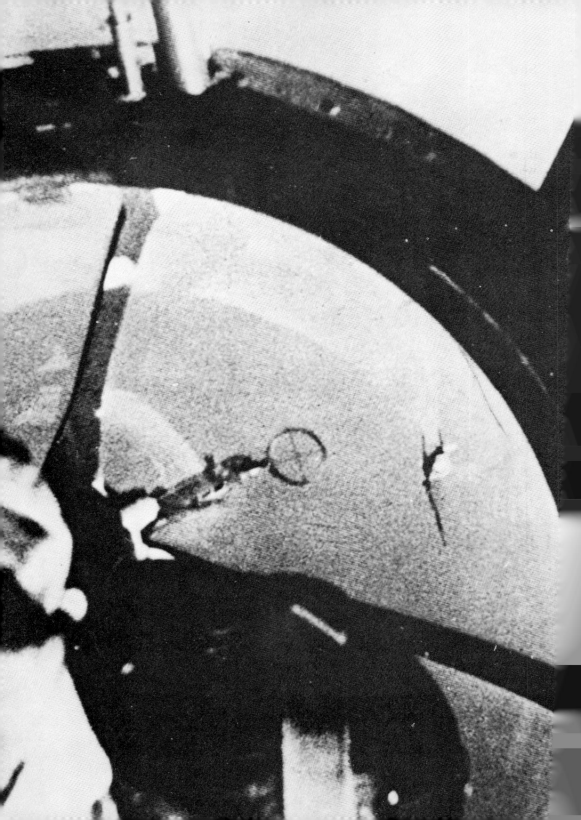

Strike Fleet closing silently upon Pearl Harbour, no attempt was made to cloak this assault movement.

So, just after noon next day, Singapore time, British pilots reported two, or possibly three, Japanese convoys about 80 miles south-east of Cambodia Point. But contact was broken in tropical rainstorms. The British found it hard to know what the warships were doing. Were they just on manoeuvres? – this seemed unlikely. Or, if they planned aggressive action, where would the attack be directed? – Thailand, Malaya, or the Dutch East Indies? The British headquarters in Singapore just ordered a general alert. It was unclear whether the situation demanded Operation "Matador", the planned move into the Kra Isthmus. *Repulse* and two destroyers had set sail for Port Darwin the previous day, 5th December.

Danger signals

News of the convoys reached London from Singapore at about 5 p.m., British time. The Chiefs of Staff hurriedly met, but after three hours the session agreed that nothing could be done without more information. The Chiefs of Staff stayed near their offices throughout the night, while in Singapore – about eight hours' time difference ahead – all possible planes were airborne, trying to regain contact with the Japanese warships.

Roosevelt heard of the first convoy sighting between 10 and 11 a.m., Washington time, 6th December. If a Japanese attack on Malaya were intended, this would certainly happen in about 14 hours, early on Sunday morning. Late during this Saturday, America's last day of peace, Roosevelt sent a personal message to Emperor Hirohito. The President knew full well that this appeal could have little effect now: "Both of us, for the sake of the peoples not only of our own countries but for the sake of humanity in neighbouring territories, have a sacred duty to restore traditional amity and prevent further death and destruction in the world."

Roosevelt appeals to Hirohito

While this message was on its way to Tokyo, where censors delayed its delivery, American signals staff began to intercept a 14-part Japanese note. This angrily rejected the last American document: "The American Government, always holding fast to unrealistic theories and refusing to yield an inch on its impractical principles, caused undue delay in the negotiations."

Diplomatic break

99

Opposite Another victim? A bomber pilot tries to get his gun-sights on an enemy aircraft

Japan's decision to break off negotiations – tantamount to a declaration of hostilities – was not given until the final section of the Note, which did not reach Washington until early on 7th December. The Japanese Ambassador was instructed to hand over the Note at 1 p.m., a clear sign that Japan meant to start hostilities at about that time. But already, after reading the first paragraphs intercepted late on the 6th, Roosevelt exclaimed: "This means war."

The President and his advisers still believed the Japanese were about to attack Thailand or Malaya. There was still no sign of an attack on American possessions. Even if American Pacific possessions were attacked, Pearl Harbour seemed a most unlikely target. Forces at this Hawaiian base were still only on "third alert," merely designed to cover sabotage attempts.

British air patrols had tried frantically to regain contact with the Japanese convoys. Meanwhile, in view of a possible naval clash, the battleship *Repulse* had been ordered back from her voyage to the safety of Port Darwin, and to make all speed to rejoin the *Prince of Wales* in Singapore waters.

Climax   Suddenly, events exploded into dreadful climax. Descriptions are complicated by the different time zones: Hawaiian time was $19\frac{1}{2}$ hours earlier than the Japanese time used by the Strike Force, and nearly six hours earlier than Washington.

Japanese land in Malaya   Just after midnight on 7/8th December, Singapore time, a short signal flashed to Singapore headquarters from Eighth Army Brigade, Kota Bharu, Malaya. Three Japanese warships were anchored off the darkened beaches and the first troops were wading ashore. Other signals reported that the Japanese were landing unopposed at the Thai ports of Singora and Patani. These were the very points where they had been expected; they would have been covered if the British had moved into the Kra Isthmus.

Towards Pearl Harbour   Already, the Japanese Strike Force for Pearl Harbour had steered south and increased speed to 26 knots. Gigantic bow waves cut through the Pacific swell and spread fluorescent spray. By 6 a.m., 7th December Hawaiian time, the carriers had reached their aircraft launching point, latitude 26° North, longitude 158° West, about 275 miles north of Oahu.

100

Technicians ran across the spray-sodden flight decks and clustered around the glistening aircraft. Pilots joked as they climbed into their cramped cockpits. Leading the raid would be Commander Fuchida Mitsuo; in recognition of this honour he wore a white headband round his helmet, as the samurai warriors had once worn; his aircraft was painted with bright red and yellow stripes. He nodded through the canopy screen; the technician swung the propellor. His aircraft thundered into life.

The first wave of aircraft screamed up from the pitching *Take-off*
decks – 40 torpedo bombers, 50 high-level bombers, 50 dive-bombers and 50 fighters. One by one they rose and grouped into formation and droned away into the magnificent sunrise for the attack on sleeping Pearl Harbour.

7 Attack

SUNDAY MORNING in Washington saw the late arrival of the last section of Tokyo's note breaking off relations with America. U.S. officials rushed this intercepted message to the White House and State Department. At the Japanese Embassy, diplomats frantically tried to prepare the note from transmission form into a proper document, suitable for handing to Cordell Hull at the 1 p.m. deadline. News of the Japanese landings in Malaya was on its way from Singapore to London. And the Japanese diplomats in Washington were already too late to hand over the final document before outbreak of war.

Commander Fuchida Mitsuo sighted the coast of Oahu Island at about 7.35 a.m. Hawaiian time, 1.05 p.m. in Washington. He gracefully banked his aircraft to the right in order to sweep down the west of the island for a southern low-level run at Pearl Harbour base. A curt order crackled over the radio from his plane: "All aircraft immediately attack enemy positions."

Pearl Harbour in sight

Moments later the Japanese raiders could see the American fleet nestled below them in Pearl Harbour. And the warships lay helplessly there, unaware, and making excellent targets in their side-by-side positions. Fuchida wrote later: "I have seen all German ships assembled in Kiel Harbour. I have also seen the French battleships in Brest. And finally I have often seen our own warships in review before the Emperor. But never, even in deepest peace, have I seen ships anchored 500 to 1,000 yards from one another (110)."

The sleeping fleet

Another Japanese pilot, Nakaya, described the astonishing

103

Opposite The U.S.S. *Arizona* reels at a crazy angle after being hit by Japanese bombs and torpedoes in the attack on the U.S. base at Pearl Harbour scene: "Pearl Harbour was still asleep in the morning mist. It was calm and serene inside the harbour, not even a trace of smoke from the ships at Oahu. The orderly groups of barracks, the wriggling white line of the automobile road climbing up to the mountain-top; fine objectives of attack in all directions. In line with these, inside the harbour, were important ships of the Pacific Fleet, strung out and anchored two ships side by side in an orderly manner (111)."

The American fleet totalled 70 combat vessels and 24 auxiliaries. The warships included 8 battleships, 2 heavy cruisers, 6 light cruisers, 29 destroyers and 5 submarines. American naval personnel were enjoying breakfast or a rest in their cabins and on the sunny decks – writing letters, reading, dozing, listening to music on the radio.

"Attack !"

At 7.49 local time Fuchida sent another order to the 182 aircraft under his command. *"To-to-to"* – "Attack! Attack! Attack!"

Down screamed the torpedo bombers to make their low-level runs across the sparkling water. The long months of planning and the years of experience in China began to pay rich dividends. The pilots knew just which targets to aim at – the mighty battleships. They could co-operate with one another with perfect cohesion. And still the Americans had to man their guns.

"Tora ! Tora !"

Only four minutes after his "attack" signal, the excited and confident Fuchida radioed the pre-arranged message for success. *"Tora! Tora! Tora!"* And his aircraft opened the devastating assault.

As the first torpedoes plunged into the Pacific and began hissing through the water towards the Pearl Harbour fleet, bombs whined down on the U.S. air fields at Hoiler Base, Hickam Field and Wheeler's Field, aimed at eliminating the fighter opposition on its own runways. Explosions ripped open the Sunday morning peace from one end of Oahu to the other. The helpless Pacific fleet suffered from simultaneous low-level torpedo attacks and medium height and dive-bombing raids, while other Japanese aircraft came hurtling in for low-level strafing sweeps to shoot up anti-aircraft positions, ground

In salvage operations at Pearl Harbour, the U.S.S. *Oklahoma*, another victim of the Japanese raid, is gradually raised from the sea-bed

installations, aircraft, and small vessels in the harbour.

Commander Ramsey, operations officer for Admiral Patrick *Alarm* Bellinger, Commander of the Hawaiian naval patrol aircraft, saw the first aircraft diving on Ford Island in the centre of Pearl Harbour. He assumed the machine to be American, piloted by some young fool "flat-hatting." Then the bomb detonated. Ramsey dashed into the radio room and ordered the alarm to be broadcast: "Air Raid Pearl Harbour. This is No Drill. Repeat. Air Raid Pearl Harbour!"

Hoarse klaxons blared. Men threw themselves behind guns and ran to ammunition stores – in some cases having to break open the doors of the latter. Five-inch anti-aircraft guns were desperately swivelled into position. And even before the first gun boomed, Ramsey's radio signal had reached Washington. But within five minutes, four American battleships had been pierced by one or more of the 1,000-lb. torpedoes sent flashing through the water. Tracks of more torpedoes criss-crossed the bay. Pearl Harbour echoed with crunching explosions, clattering machine guns, whistling, roaring bombs, and staccato anti-aircraft fire. America had at last entered the Second World War. Japanese aircraft swooped and dipped and screeched through the billowing black smoke. Flames gushed high into the air. Oil spread thick over the water.

Washington shocked

The first report of the attack to reach Washington was rushed to Admiral Stark, who immediately called the Navy Secretary, Frank Knox. For a moment Knox refused to believe the terrible news. "They must mean the Philippines!" he exclaimed. Roosevelt received the news at 1.47 p.m. Washington time, 8.17 a.m. in Oahu.

Terrible losses

The attack had been in progress for 25 minutes. And at this moment the 32,600 ton battleship *Arizona* received lethal hits. Torpedoes had already ripped through the hull, and a bomb had exploded in the forward magazines, shooting flames 500 feet into the air. Now a second bomb dropped directly down her chimney-stack, a third hit the boat deck, a fourth the No. 4 turret and four more ripped the superstructure. Flames roared along the warship. And more than 1,100 men perished on this one vessel alone, burned to death or trapped below until they drowned.

Also hit early in the battle was the battleship *Oklahoma*, torn by three torpedoes as the alarm klaxons still sounded. She began to list, and her men were ordered to climb over the starboard side as she rolled. Two more torpedoes slammed into her as she started to capsize. Men were machine-gunned as they crawled hopelessly over the hull. The battleship stopped rolling when her masts snagged the mud of the harbour bottom. More than 400 men died, and others were trapped under the hull – 32 were later released through holes cut with torches into the bottom plates.

The *West Virginia,* moored near the *Oklahoma* and alongside the *Tennessee,* received rapid torpedo hits which knocked out power, light, and communications, and the ship listed so badly that the starboard guns could only be fired by one man holding

After the Japanese attack a ship lies on its side beside the quay and dark smoke billows from the burning fuel stores

up another as ammunition was passed to the loaders. The ship had to be abandoned with fire gushing through the superstructure. By then the vessel had come to rest on the harbour bed. Salvage crews who later raised the battleship found a fearful diary scratched on a bulkhead by three trapped men who had taken 16 days to die.

And so the carnage continued. Ship after ship received direct hits or crippling blows. Ninety-five minutes after the first attack, a second wave of bombers and fighters stabbed into the attack. By now the Americans fought back with all available weapons, and the 170 aircraft in the second enemy strike could no longer expect easy runs at their targets.

Chief Flight Petty Officer Juzo Mori, pilot of a torpedo bomber, gave this eyewitness account: "The assigned objectives

A Japanese eyewitness 107

Overleaf Firefighting tenders and rescue vessels are impotent in the face of the massive destruction at Pearl Harbour

of the *Soryu* torpedo-bombers were the American battleships which we expected to find anchored along the wharf of the Oahu Naval Arsenal. We dropped in for our attack at high speed and low altitude and, when I was almost in position to release my own torpedo, I realized that the enemy warship toward which I was headed was not a battleship at all, but a cruiser . . . I did not expect to survive this attack, since I and all the other pilots anticipated heavy enemy resistance. If I were going to die, I thought, at least I wanted to know that I had torpedoed an American battleship.

"The attack of the *Soryu's* planes was met with intense anti-aircraft fire from the enemy fleet, since the bombing waves from the *Akagi* and the *Kaga* had already passed over. My bomber shook and vibrated from the impact of enemy machine-gun bullets and shrapnel. Despite my intention of swinging away from the cruiser, now dead ahead of my aircraft, and attacking the group of battleships anchored near Ford Island, I was forced to fly directly forward into a murderous rain of anti-aircraft fire . . .

"The anti-aircraft fire did not seem to affect the plane's performance, and I chose as my new objective a battleship anchored some distance from the main group of vessels . . . I swung low and put my plane into a satisfactory torpedoing position. It was imperative that my bombing approach be absolutely correct . . . By this time I was hardly conscious of what I was doing. I was reacting from habit instilled by long training, moving like an automaton.

"3,000 feet! 2,500 feet! 2,000 feet! Suddenly the battleship appeared to have leaped forward directly in front of my speeding plane; it towered ahead of the bomber like a great mountain peak.

"Prepare for release . . . Stand by!

"*Release torpedo!*

"All this time I was oblivious of the enemy's anti-aircraft fire and the distracting thunder of my plane's motor. I concentrated on nothing but the approach and the torpedo release. At the right moment I pulled back on the release with all my strength. The plane lurched and faltered as flak struck the wings and

Behind the listing battleship *California* shore installations blaze at Pearl Harbour

fuselage; my head snapped back and I felt as though a heavy beam had struck against my head.

"But – I've got it! A perfect release!

"And the plane is still flying! . . . Now that the attack was over, I was acutely conscious that the enemy anti-aircraft fire was bracketing and smashing into my bomber. The enemy shells appeared to be coming from all directions, and I was so frightened that before I left the target area my clothes were soaking with sweat . . . (112)"

By 10 a.m. local time the attack was over. Commander Fuchida, who had circled overhead to watch the progress of the second strike, banked his aircraft and headed back to the carrier force. The drone of the enemy formations dwindled over the horizon. They left behind a scene of the most horrible chaos: crackling flames, screaming moaning men, hissing steam. Warships lay submerged up to their superstructures, or overturned, or tilting at crazy angles. Shattered hangers and buildings spread their smoking rubble across the dock roads. Wreckage and bodies floated in the oil-scummed sea. The Americans counted the terrible cost: five battleships, three destroyers, a

Scene of chaos

In a terrifying confusion of exploding shells, the U.S.S. *Shaw* blows up
after a direct Japanese hit on her ammunition store

minelayer, and almost 200 aircraft, including at least 112 out of
148 good Navy combat aircraft and 52 out of 148 serviceable
Army fighters and bombers. Only 38 American aircraft had
been able to claw up into the air, and ten of these had been shot
down. More than 2,000 American sailors, 109 Marines, 218
soldiers and 68 civilians had died, or would do so as a result of
their ghastly wounds.

Hull's anger   In Washington, Nomura and Kurusu had delivered their last
diplomatic note – which, due to the inefficiency in the Embassy,
had been handed over at 1.47 p.m. instead of 1.00 p.m., and so
after the American leaders had heard the news of Pearl Harbour.
Hull had flung the paper upon his desk and had shouted to the
Japanese envoys: "In all my fifty years of public service, I have
never seen a document that was more crowded with infamous
falsehoods and distortions – infamous falsehoods and distortions on a scale so huge that I never imagined until today that
any government on this planet was capable of uttering them
(113)."

Yet despite Hull's justifiable treatment of the Japanese
Ambassador, Japan's initial victory seemed complete. The U.S.
Pacific Fleet had been shattered to an extent that even Tokyo
had never dreamed possible. Japanese troops swept on through
Thailand and Malaya. The Philippines would soon be overrun.

A ship's boat is lowered in an attempt to find more survivors from the British ships *Repulse* and *Prince of Wales*, sunk by the Japanese

News reaches Churchill

And on 11th December, Winston Churchill received an appalling telephone call, which he described in his memoirs: "It was the First Sea Lord. His voice sounded odd. He gave a sort of cough and gulp, and at first I could not hear quite clearly. 'Prime Minister, I have to report to you that the *Prince of Wales* and the *Repulse* have both been sunk by the Japanese – we think by aircraft . . .' 'Are you sure it's true?' 'There is no doubt at all.' So I put the telephone down. I was thankful to be alone. In all the war I never received a more direct shock . . . As I turned and twisted in bed the full horror of the news sank in upon me. There were no British or American capital ships in the Indian Ocean or the Pacific except the American survivors of Pearl Harbour, who were hastening back to California. Over all this vast expanse of waters Japan was supreme, and we everywhere were weak and naked . . . (114)"

More than 1,000 men on board the *Prince of Wales* and *Repulse* had been drowned, including the Commander-in-Chief, Admiral Sir Tom Phillips. So much for the British deterrent, which had paid so dearly for insufficient air cover. Only a few weeks later Singapore and Hong Kong fell into Japanese hands, then Java. Everywhere, through a mixture of brilliant preparation, meticulous execution, cruel ruthlessness – and allied weaknesses – the Japanese battle plans had been accomplished.

113

In the eerie light of the moon, a battle squadron moves to a new position
in the Pacific

8 Aftermath

British relief

THE REACTION of Winston Churchill and his Ministers to the first news of the Pearl Harbour disaster seems at first glance to be astonishingly callous: Churchill felt "the greatest joy." Anthony Eden, the Foreign Secretary, wrote: "I could not conceal my relief, and did not have to try." Other British political and military chiefs felt the same. This elation remained even when the full details of the Pearl Harbour loss reached London, even after the dreadful news of the *Prince of Wales* and *Repulse* sinkings. For America was now in the war.

Churchill, on hearing the Pearl Harbour report, at once telephoned President Roosevelt. The American leader declared: "We are all in the same boat now." No longer would Britain have to fight with only the struggling Soviets as an active ally. America, with her potentially vast military power, had joined the contest. Time would be needed for this strength to be accumulated and applied, but whereas Axis power would be whittled away, Allied forces would multiply. As Eden commented: "I felt that whatever happened now, it was only a question of time."

Churchill exclaimed in his *Memoirs*: "So we had won after all! Yes, after Dunkirk; after the fall of France . . . after the threat of invasion. . . . We had won the war. England would live; Britain would live; the Commonwealth of Nations and the Empire would live. How long the war would last or in what fashion it would end no man could tell, nor did I at this moment care. Once again in our long Island history we should emerge, however mauled or mutilated, safe and victorious (115)."

U.S.S. *Texas* fires a broadside at an enemy ship

Churchill's satisfaction showed in the relish with which he worded Britain's official declaration of war against Japan. The document handed to the Japanese Ambassador was larded thick with lavish courtesy: ". . . In view of these wanton acts of unprovoked aggression committed in flagrant violation of International Law and particularly Article 1 of the Third Hague Convention relative to the opening of hostilities, to which both Japan and the United Kingdom are parties, His Majesty's Ambassador at Tokyo has been instructed to inform the Imperial Japanese Government in the name of His Majesty's Government in the United Kingdom that a state of war exists between our two countries. I have the honour to be . . ., Sir, Your Obedient Servant, Winston S. Churchill."

As Churchill commented: "Some people did not like this ceremonial style. But after all when you have to kill a man it costs nothing to be polite (116)."

Tokyo's warmongers hoped America would be so shocked and shattered by the initial defeats, and by Japan's rapid conquests, that she would seek a return to the negotiating table, to Japan's advantage. But some enemy military chiefs did perceive that a prolonged war could only be disastrous. Even Admiral Yamamoto, architect of Pearl Harbour, told Prince Konoye: "If I am told to fight regardless of consequence, I shall run wild considerably for the first six months or a year, but I have utterly no confidence for the second and third years (117)."

Pearl Harbour inflamed the Japanese spirits of *Hakko Ichiu* and *Bushido*, as echoed in the Emperor's broadcast on the morning of the attack: "The hallowed spirits of Our Imperial Ancestors guard Us from above. We rely upon the loyalty and courage of Our subjects in Our confident expectation that the task bequeathed by Our Forefathers will be carried forward, and that the source of evil will be speedily eradicated and an enduring peace immutably established in East Asia, preserving thereby the glory of Our Empire." *Japanese spirit*

But if Pearl Harbour had boosted Japanese ego, the attack had also thrown Americans into black and violent rage. If the Emperor's flowery words summed up the typical Japanese attitude, American feelings were typified by this down-to-earth comment from Admiral Halsey, who returned to Pearl Harbour with the carrier *Enterprise* on 8th December. "Before we're through with them, the Japanese language will be spoken only in hell." *American rage*

Halsey's return was significant: America had suffered grievously at Pearl Harbour. But at least her aircraft carriers had escaped in time. These warships were to prove even more important in the Pacific fighting than battleships. Symbolic, too, was the fate of the Japanese warships in the Strike Force used for the attack on Pearl Harbour: although they now sailed victorious, only one, a destroyer, would still be afloat at the end of the war. Four of the carriers would be sunk at the Battle of Midway, the other two in 1944 and the two battleships at Guadalcanal.

Never before had a nation started a war with such colossal victories. Yet in August, 1945, this same nation would suffer the most shattering defeat in the history of man, when the first atomic bombs exploded upon Hiroshima and Nagasaki. This was to be the terrible price of Pearl Harbour. *Towards Hiroshima*

117

Overleaf The war with Japan opened with a terrible bombing raid, but it ended with an even more terrible raid – the dropping of the atomic bombs on Hiroshima and Nagasaki

Table of Dates

1922
6th February   Nine-Power treaty

1937
July   Japan invades China
12th December   Sinking of *U.S.S. Panay*

1938
December   Japanese policy statement on "New Order in East Asia"

1939
August   Japan renounces Anti-Comintern Pact
September   Outbreak of war in the West

1940
April   Denmark and Norway occupied by Germans
May   British army evacuated from Dunkirk
10th June   Italy enters war
17th June   France sues for peace
27th July   Japanese policy statement issued
29th August   French agree to Japanese moves into south Indochina
22nd September   Japanese overrun Indochina
27th September   Tripartite Pact signed by Japan, Italy and Germany

1941
16th January   U.S. Plan Dog Directive issued
March   Japanese Foreign Minister visits Moscow and Berlin

11th March	Lend-Lease Bill becomes law
27th March	Anglo-U.S. ABC-1 plan
22nd June	Germany invades Russia
9th August	Churchill-Roosevelt meeting
6th September	Japanese policy document on "The Essentials for Carrying Out the Empire's Policies"
13th October	Tojo becomes Japanese Prime Minister
25th October	*Prince of Wales* leaves for Cape Town
1st November	Japanese Liaison Conference decides date for war; Admiral Yamamoto submits offensive plans
4th November	Japanese Imperial Conference ratifies war decision
7th November	Japanese Ambassador presents Proposal A in Washington
16th November	Americans reject Proposal A
18th November	Japanese strike force sails from Kure for Pearl Harbour
20th November	Japanese present final demands—Proposal B
26th November	Americans reject Proposal B
27th November	U.S. forces alerted
2nd December	*Prince of Wales* and *Repulse* reach Singapore
5th December	Japanese task force moves on Thailand and Malaya
7th December	Pearl Harbour (8th December, Japanese time)
11th December	*Prince of Wales* and *Repulse* sunk

Glossary

AMPHIBIOUS Designed to operate both on land and in water.

ANTI-AIRCRAFT Relating to defence against aircraft attack.

ANTI-TANK Relating to defence against armoured vehicles.

ARMISTICE An agreement between opposing armies to suspend fighting in order to discuss peace terms.

ATTACHES Specialists attached to a diplomatic mission.

ATTRITION Constant wearing down to weaken or destroy.

AUGMENTED Increased in size or strength.

AXIS The alliance of Nazi Germany, Fascist Italy and Japan, established in 1936 and defeated in the Second World War.

BELLIGERENT Aggressive.

BLITZKREIG An intensive military attack designed to defeat the opposition quickly.

BRINKMANSHIP The art of pushing a dangerous situation to the limit of safety and peace in order to win an advantage.

COLLABORATION To work with others on a joint project.

CYPHERS Secret messages; the key to secret messages.

DETERRENT A weapon held by one state to discourage attack by another, usually by instilling fear.

DIGNITARIES People of high official rank in government.

DRAFT An outline of a document.

EMBARGO A stoppage of commerce by government order.

FLAK Anti-aircraft fire or artillery.

GARRISON Troops who guard a fortified place.

GUERILLA WARFARE War between regular forces, such as the army, and an irregular, usually politically motivated, armed force.

LIST To lean to one side.

LUFTWAFFE The German airforce.

MANDATE Support given to a government and its policies through electoral victory; an official command.

MEDIATE   To bring about an agreement between opposing sides; to resolve differences.

MODUS VIVENDI   A practical compromise between conflicting interests.

PARLEYS   Discussions between enemies under a truce to decide terms of surrender.

RETALIATORY   Punishing someone by returning an injury or wrong.

SQUADRON   A subdivision of a naval fleet.

STOCKPILE   A large store or supply, for future use.

WRESTED   Forcibly seized by violent or unlawful means.

Further Reading

Bergamini, David, *Japan's Imperial Conspiracy* (London, 1971)

British War Cabinet Papers, Public Records Office (London)

Butow, Robert, *Tojo and the Coming of the War* (Princeton, 1961)

Churchill, Sir Winston, *The Second World War*, vols. II and III (London, 1949, 1950)

Craigie, Sir Robert, *Behind the Japanese Mask* (London, 1945)

Eden, Anthony (Lord Avon), *The Reckoning* (London, 1965)

Feis, Herbert, *Road to Pearl Harbour* (Princeton, 1950)

Foreign Relations of United States (Japan, 1931–1941; US Government Printing Office, 1943)

Grew, Joseph, *Ten Years in Japan* (New York, 1944)

Gwyer, J. M. A. and Butler, J. R. M., *Grand Strategy*, volume III, British Official War History series, (HMSO, London, 1964)

Harris, Nathaniel, *Pearl Harbour* (London, Batsford, 1986)

Hearings before the Joint Committee on the Pearl Harbour attack (U.S. Government Printing Office, 1946)

Hull, Cordell, *Memoirs* (London, 1959)

Ike, Nobutaka (ed. and trans.), *Japan's Decision for War, Records of the 1941 Policy Conferences* (Stanford, 1967)

Okumiya, M. and Horikoshi, J. (with Caidin, M.), *Zero!* (London, 1957)

Mao Tse-tung, *On Protracted War* (Peking, 1966)

Millis, Walter, *This is Pearl!* (New York, 1947)

Morison, S. E., *The Rising Sun in the Pacific*, History of US Navy operations in World War II, Vol. III, 1931–April, 1942 (London, 1948)

Morton, Louis, *The War in the Pacific*, US Army in World War II (US Army Department, 1962)

Potter, John Deane, *Yamamoto: The Man Who Menaced America* (New York, 1965)

Roosevelt, Elliott (ed.), *FDR – His Personal Letters, 1928–1945* (New York, 1950)

Trevor-Roper, Hugh (ed.), *Hitler's War Directives* (London, 1964)

Wohlstetter, Roberta, *Pearl Harbour, Warning and Decision* (Stanford, 1962)

Woodward, Sir Llewelyn, *British Foreign Policy in the Second World War* (HMSO, London, 1962)

List of Sources

(1) Okumiya, *Zero!* 39
(2) Bergamini, *Japan's Imperial Conspiracy*. 285
(3) *British and Foreign State Papers*, cxl., 1936
(4) Morison, *History of US Navy Operations*. 14
(5) Mao Tse-tung, *On Protracted War*
(6) Okumiya, *op. cit.*, 15
(7) *Ibid*, 33
(8) Morison, *op. cit.*, 83
(9) Okumiya, *op cit.*, 16
(10) Morison, *op. cit.*, 83
(11) Ike, *Japan's Decision for War*, xvi
(12) Morton, *US Army in World War II*. 71
(13) *Ibid*, 75, 76
(14) Churchill, *The Second World War*, II, 166–167
(15) Morton, *op. cit.*, 76
(16) Feis, *Road to Pearl Harbour*, 87
(17) House of Commons Debates, Vol. 362, col. 60
(18) Churchill, *op. cit.*, 199–200
(19) Morton, *op. cit.*, 78, 79
(20) Feis, *op. cit.*, 95
(21) *Ibid*
(22) Ike, *op. cit.*, 4–13
(23) *British War Cabinet papers*, file number CAB 65/9
(24) Hull, *Memoirs*, I, 906
(25) *British War Cabinet Papers*, file number
(26) Morton, *op. cit.*, 81, 82
(27) *British War Cabinet papers*, file number CAB 65/10
(28) Morton, *op. cit.*, 87
(29) *Hearings before the Joint Committee*, part 15, 1941
(30) Trevor-Roper, *Hitler's War Directives*
(31) Wohlstetter, *Pearl Harbour*, 69
(32) *British War Cabinet Papers* (Defence Committee), file number CAB 69/8
(33) Eden, *The Reckoning*, 308, 309; Churchill, *op. cit.*, III, 157
(34) Ike, *op. cit.*, 22
(35) *British War Cabinet papers* (Defence Committee) file number CAB 69/2
(36) Ike, *op. cit.*, 29, 30
(37) *Ibid*, 37, 38
(38) *Ibid*, 49, 50
(39) *Ibid*, 54, 55, 56
(40) Morton, *op. cit.*, 93
(41) Ike, *op. cit.*, 59
(42) *Ibid*, 61, 64
(43) *Ibid*, 66
(44) *Hearings* (*Op. cit.*), part 20, 93
(45) *Foreign Relations of United States, Japan*, 485–86
(46) Ike, *op. cit.*, 97
(47) *Ibid*, 100
(48) *Ibid*, 106
(49) *Hearings* (*op. cit.*), part 12, 165
(50) Ike, *op. cit.*, 119
(51) *Hearings* (*op. cit.*), part 12, 17
(52) Gwyer, *Grand Strategy*. III, 132
(53) *Ibid*, 133
(54) Churchill, *op. cit.*, III, 390
(55) Woodward, *British Foreign Policy*, 176
(56) *British War Cabinet papers* (Chiefs of Staff Committee), file number CAB 79/13
(57) Ike, *op. cit.*, 127
(58) *Ibid*, 135, 136
(59) *Ibid*, 153–155

(60) *Hearings* (*op. cit.*), part 12, 261
(61) Eden, *op. cit.*, 313
(62) Gwyer, *op. cit.*, 281
(63) Ike, *op. cit.*, 179, 180
(64) *Hearings* (*op. cit.*), part 12, 64
(65) *Ibid.* 66
(66) Ike, *op. cit.*, 185
(67) *British War Cabinet papers* (Defence Committee), file number CAB 69/2
(68) *Ibid*
(69) Ike, *op. cit.*, 186
(70) *British War Cabinet papers*, file number CAB 65/24
(71) Ike, *op. cit.*, 202–204
(72) Morison, *op. cit.*, 85, 86
(73) *Hearings* (*op. cit.*), part 12, 90
(74) *Ibid*, part 14, 1064
(75) Bergamini, *op. cit.*, 807
(76) *Hearings* (*op. cit.*), part 14, 1056
(77) *Ibid*, part 12, 92
(78) Ike, *op. cit.*, 232–233
(79) *Ibid.* 239
(80) *British War Cabinet papers*, file number CAB 65/24
(81) Gwyer, *op. cit.*, 257
(82) *Hearings* (*op. cit.*), part 12, 100
(83) *Ibid.* 99
(84) Morison, *op. cit.*, 86, 97
(85) *Hearings* (*op. cit.*), part 12, 116
(86) Ike, *op. cit.*, 246
(87) *Hearings* (*op. cit.*), part 12, 137
(88) *Ibid.* 154
(89) *Foreign Relations of US* (*op. cit.*), II, 755
(90) Hull, *op. cit.*, II, 1070
(91) *Hearings* (*op. cit.*), part 14, 1113–1115
(92) *Ibid.* 1123
(93) *Ibid*, part 12, 165
(94) *Ibid*, part 14, 1405
(95) Roosevelt, *FDR – His Personal Letters*, II, 1246
(96) Churchill, *op. cit.*, III, 530
(97) Hearings (*op. cit.*), part 11, 5433
(98) *Ibid.* part 20, 4473
(99) *Ibid.* part 11, 5433
(100) *Ibid.* 5434
(101) *Foreign Relations of US* (*op. cit.*), II, 769
(102) *Hearings* (*op. cit.*), part 14, 1083
(103) *Ibid.* 1406
(104) *Ibid*, part 12, 10430
(105) *Ibid*, part 14, 1407
(106) *British War Cabinet Papers*, file number CAB 65/24
(107) *Hearings* (*op. cit.*), part 17, 2636
(108) *Ibid*, part 14, 1407
(109) *British War Cabinet papers*, file number CAB 65/24
(110) Potter, *Yamamoto*, 98
(111) Morison, *op. cit.*, 94, 95
(112) Okumiya, *op. cit.*, 45–47
(113) Bergamini, *op. cit.*, 848
(114) Churchill, *op. cit.*, III, 551
(115) *Ibid.* 539
(116) *Ibid.* 542, 543
(117) Memoirs of Prince Konoye, translated from extracts printed in *Asahi Shimbun*, December 1945

Index

127

Picture Credits

The Author and Publishers wish to thank all those who have given permission for the reproduction of illustrations in this book: Conway Picture Library, *frontispiece*, 32–33, 42–43, 50–51, 105, 111, 114, 116; International News Photos, 28, 90; Keystone Press, 10, 16–17, 22–23, 26–27, 38–39, 46, 56–57, 60, 70, 74–75, 78, 81, 93, 96–97, 98, 102, 107, 108–109, 114, 115, 118. The map on pp. 64–65 is reproduced from Martin Gilbert's *Recent History Atlas* (1966) by kind permission of the publishers, Weidenfeld and Nicolson Ltd. The jacket picture is reproduced by courtesy of the National Maritime Museum, London (Estate of Norman Wilkinson).